TABLE OF CONTENTS

INTRODUCTION

INTRODUCTION

The Myers-Briggs Personality system is made up of 16 different types. This book covers each type. It is easy to find out your Myers-Briggs type (which is a four-letter code) using the internet by typing "MBTI Test" (MBTI is an abbreviation for Myers-Briggs Personality Test) in the search engine or you can go to my personal favorite – www.16personalities.com to take the test for free. However, my hope is that after reading this book, you will be able to identify either yourself and/or the people you see every day as a particular Myers-Briggs type.

Do you ever wonder why people act the way they do? In this book of Personality Insider, the behavior of each Myers-Briggs type will be explained and, more importantly, simplified. As a student of the system for several years, I have created the "Education Model" to help you better understand how each personality type's personality traits show up in the world. Before we get to the new way of decoding the Myers-Briggs system, the traditional and not completely accurate model of the system must be addressed.

The Incomplete Myers-Briggs Model

The four-letter labels of a personality for all 16 different types, such as "ENTJ," "ISTP," "INFP," etc., are derived from the often confusing, incomplete yet traditional way of looking at the Myers-Briggs personality system. Addressing, what I call, the "Incomplete Myers-Briggs Model" is designed to give you the reasoning behind the "four-letter code" that classifies each personality type. This is the only time in this book that this method of viewing the system will be addressed because the Education Model is much easier to understand and apply to everyday life. Here is a visual of the model:

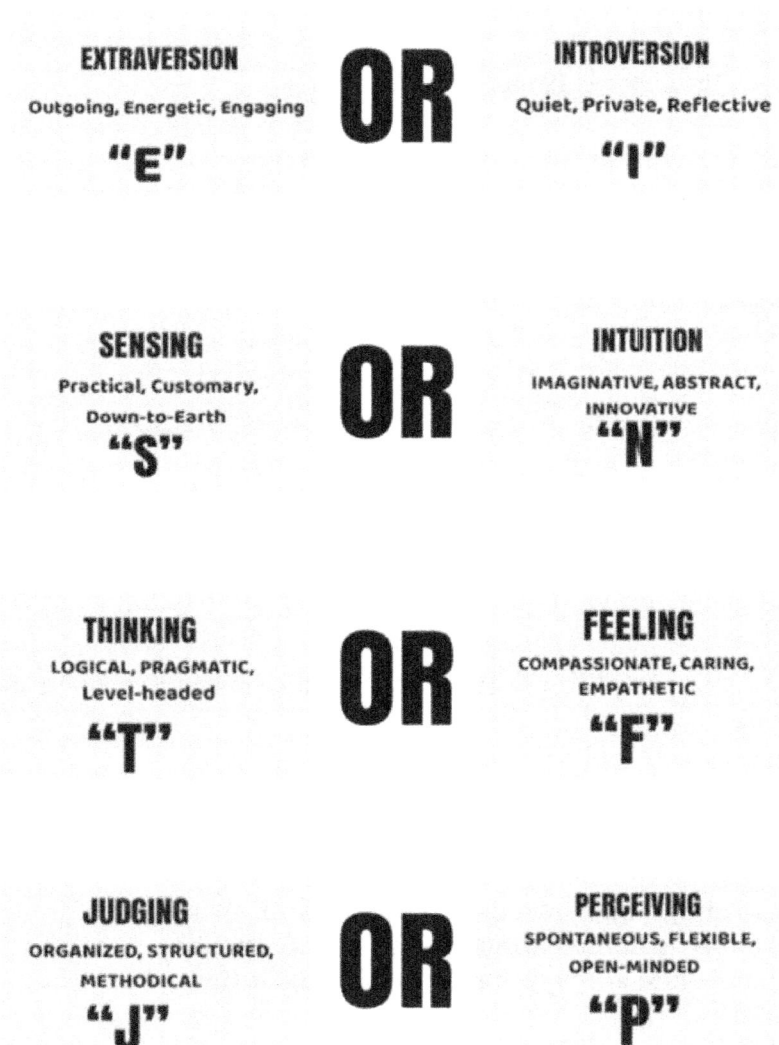

We all prefer to operate with one cognitive function of the following four categories:

1. **Extroversion vs. Introversion**

2. **Intuition vs. Sensing**

3. **Thinking vs. Feeling**

4. **Judging vs. Perceiving**

The Eight Cognitive Functions in Each Category

Extroversion = you prefer to gain energy by being around other people.

Introversion= you prefer to gain energy by not being around other people.

Intuition= you prefer to process information in abstract, theoretical terms.

Sensing= you prefer to process information in practical, concrete terms.

Thinking= you prefer to prioritize logic over compassion when making decisions.

Feeling= you prefer to prioritize compassion over logic when making decisions.

Judging= you prefer to have a systematic, methodical lifestyle.

Perceiving= you prefer to have a spontaneous, open-ended lifestyle.

When reading about Myers-Briggs, you will always see a four-letter code. That is an abbreviation for four of the eight cognitive functions a particular personality type prefers when making decisions. They are abbreviated as follows:

Extroversion = E

Introversion = I

Intuition = N

Sensing = S

Thinking = T

Feeling= F

Judging= J

Perceiving= P

For example, if one were to prefer extroversion over introversion, intuition over sensing, feeling over thinking, and perceiving over judging, that would make them an ENFP once abbreviated.

Confused yet? I certainly was when I read this traditional way of looking at Myers-Briggs. It makes sense on the surface once you have reread it a few times over, but it simply does not address how absolutely everyone is capable of introversion, extraversion, sensing, intuition, thinking, feeling, judging, and perceiving. This is the reason I call it the INCOMPLETE Myers-Briggs Model. It does not address how humans are capable of all the things I mentioned above.

Although the Incomplete Myers-Briggs Model does not cover the "full story," it does have two key components that are still applicable for the new way of looking at the personality system. Therefore, the new way of looking at Myers-Briggs that is addressed in this book can only be understood if the two following components of the model are not applied:

1. The Incomplete Myers-Briggs Model explains the origins of the four-letter code (again, ESFP, ISTP, INTJ...etc.)

2. A person does prefer one cognitive function over the other (kind of like how you prefer to use your left or right hand even though you could technically use both); however, it does nothing to explain how each cognitive function preference affects their personality. Again, this is why I call it INCOMPLETE yet necessary from a prerequisite standpoint for learning the Myers-Briggs Education Model.

The Myers-Briggs Education Model: A New, Simplified Theory

There are four cognitive functions that each of the 16 Myers-Briggs personality types uses. There are eight total cognitive functions; therefore, each type uses four of them in their mental processes and the other four cognitive functions are complete "blind spots" for each type.

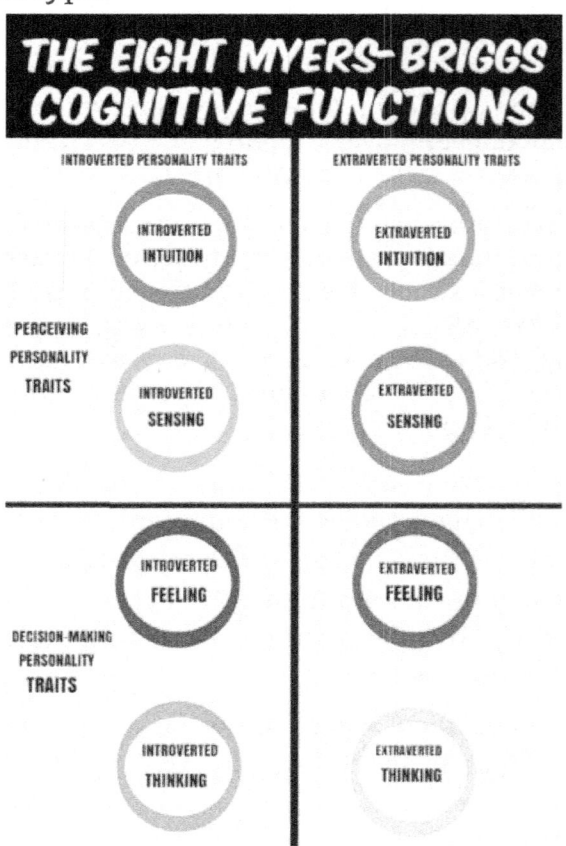

The following are the eight cognitive functions and the nicknames I have given each to simplify and make each way of thinking identifiable. Going forward, to make things simple in this book, I will be calling the cognitive functions "personality traits" instead. I think it is a fair, simplified synonym.

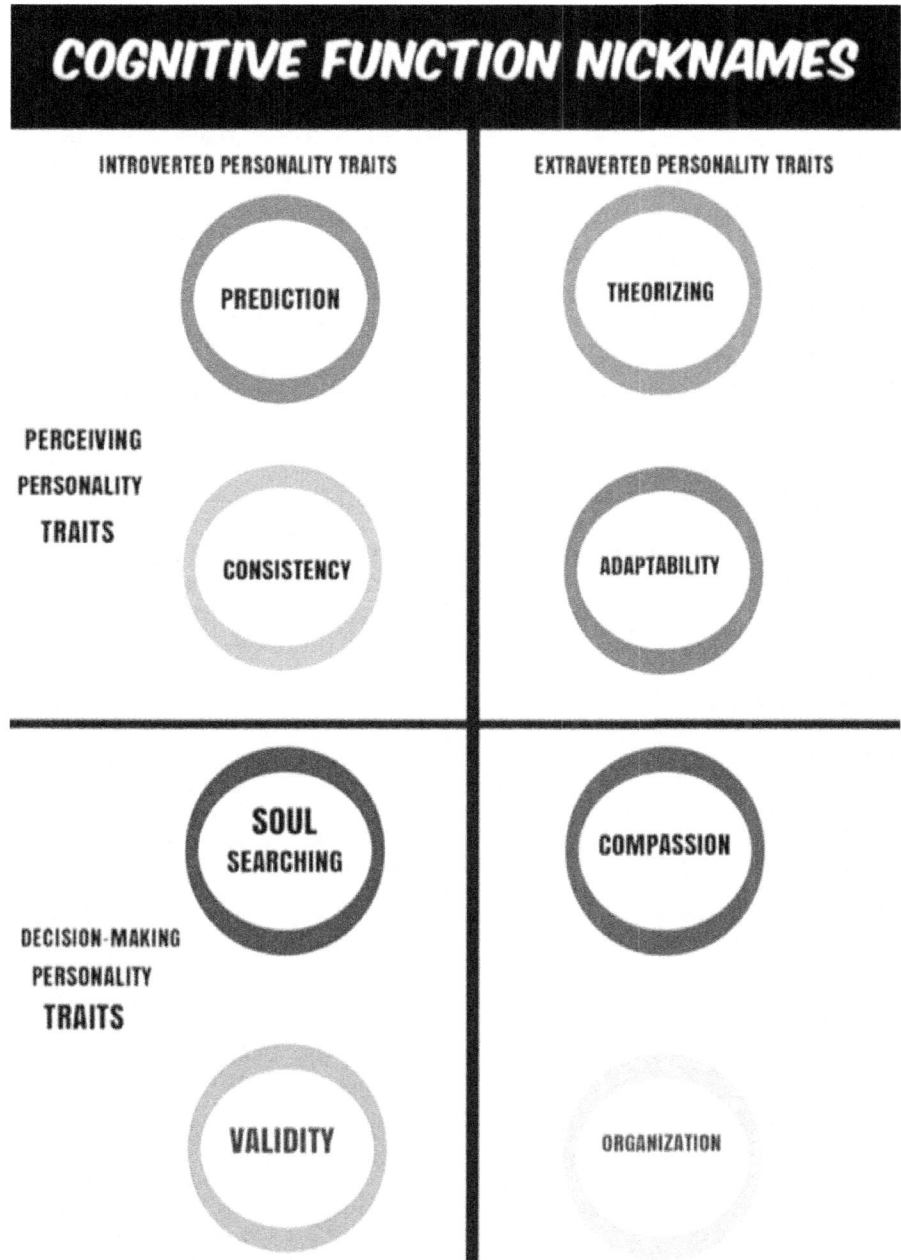

Extraverted Sensing – Adaptability

I chose the nickname "Adaptability" for Extraverted Sensing because it is a personality trait that is very physically adaptive to its environment. People who have this trait as a strength are very "in-tune" with their body and the way it interacts with the physical environment. The types that use this trait also seek satisfaction and thrill from "hands-on" activities. Some more obvious examples of this are riding a motorcycle and painting. This trait also is very risk-taking, fun, and spontaneous.

Extraverted Intuition – Theorizing

I chose the nickname "Theorizing" for Extraverted Intuition because it is a trait that makes intuitive and uncanny observations regarding the external environment. The Theorizing personality trait can draw connections, patterns, and ideas into a creative drive that, at its core, asks, "What could be?" It seeks many ways of accomplishing something. Some obvious examples of this are stand-up comedy (which is Theorizing in a humorous way about the external environment) and entrepreneurship (which scans the external sphere for ideas and connections that could improve society).

Introverted Sensing – Consistency

I chose Consistency as a nickname for Introverted Sensing because it is a trait that reminisces on personal experience to perceive the world. It is affiliated with routine, consistency, tradition, and memory of the past in concrete, practical terms. Some obvious examples of this are reliable data entry and pride in family traditions.

Introverted Intuition – Prediction

I chose Prediction for Introverted Intuition because it is a trait that focuses on "what will be" based on personal insight. It is a perceiving personality trait that finds the best way of accomplishing things. It also considers how other individuals would perceive different solutions. Some more obvious examples of this are data forecasting and improving on proven business models.

Extraverted Feeling – Compassion

I chose Compassion for the Extraverted Feeling personality trait because it is focused on making sure those around you are happy and satisfied. People that have this personality trait are able to sense the feelings of those around them. Some more obvious examples of this trait are a nurse tending to a patient or doing a good deed for a homeless person.

Introverted Feeling – Soul Searching

I chose Soul Searching for Introverted Feeling because it seeks to understand the emotions of the self and others. It very much is a personal value system that attempts to delineate what is "right" and "wrong" when it comes to the treatment of the self and others. It has an uncanny ability to empathize with any emotion through deep, quick self-reflection. The Compassion trait seeks to make another person feel better while the Soul Searching trait seeks to understand how another person feels. Some more obvious examples of this is a therapist seeking ways to help a client or an actor/actress being able to express any emotion in a role they're playing.

Extraverted Thinking – Organization

I chose Organization for Extraverted Thinking because it is a personality trait that seeks effectiveness for the self and others. People with this trait are very good at organizing their external environment in a way that is logically beneficial for all involved. Some more obvious examples of this are managing a company and implementing linear logic for well-refined systems that accomplish tasks.

Introverted Thinking – Validity

I chose Validity for Introverted Thinking because it is a personality trait that seeks to analyze what is individually valid to the person using it. It is not concerned with typical, conforming logic like Organization. It is a personalized logic that looks at every perspective of a situation. Some more obvious examples of this are scientists, general contractors, and unique, logical debating tactics to prove a point in public discourse.

Now that you are familiar with the nicknames for each personality trait in the Myers-Briggs Personality System, it is now pertinent to discuss the types that use each trait. It is also important to note that even though some types use particular traits, it does not necessarily mean they are talented at using that particular personality trait.

Conveniently, the Education Model makes it easy to determine each type's personality trait strengths and weaknesses.

Each personality type has four different personality traits. They have one that is their "superpower" or leading personality trait that they typically use 50% of the time or more when engaging with the world. In the Education Model, I have assigned this personality trait as a "PhD" because if a personality type has a "PhD" in a particular personality trait, it means they are an expert at utilizing that personality trait.

Secondly, I have assigned the personality trait that each personality type uses 35% of the time or more as a "Bachelor's Degree." If a personality type has a Bachelor's Degree in a personality trait, it means they will become a more well-rounded, integrated, happy, and healthier individual the more they use it in their daily lives.

Thirdly, I have assigned the personality trait that each type uses 10% of the time or more as the "High School Diploma." If a personality type is using this trait, it means they are under stress. They need to be more "educated" in developing this trait, which is why it is called a High School Diploma. Under stress, it is more tempting and easier to jump to this personality trait instead of the Bachelor's Degree. The High School Diploma trait can be developed and become less of a challenge with healthy stress management and life experience.

Finally, I have assigned the personality trait each type uses 5% of the time or more as "Elementary Education." This trait only shows up under extreme stress. It is very difficult for each type to develop it because it is very immature, sporadic, and subconscious. However, with self-awareness, life experience, and processing pain positively, it can be developed.

In summation, each Myers-Briggs personality type uses four of the eight personality traits. The four that are not used are blind spots to each type. The four used are assigned different skill levels for each type through the Education Model.

Those education "degrees" or "skills" are:

1. PhD: The expert or "superpower" personality trait

2. Bachelor's Degree: The personality trait that leads to personal growth and satisfaction

3. High School Diploma: The personality trait that shows up under stress

4. The Elementary Education: The personality trait that shows up under severe stress.

Again, both the High School Diploma and Elementary Education can be developed through proper stress-reduction techniques; however, each personality type will be happier, more satisfied, and grounded in their identity if they spend almost all of their time using their PhD and Bachelor's Degree personality traits.

With all this being said, I will now break down each personality type's Education Model so you can have a simplified and easy way of understanding the 16 different Myers-Briggs Personality Types.

1. INTP

INTP Education Model	
PhD	Validity
Bachelor's Degree	Theorizing
High School Diploma	Consistency
Elementary Education	Compassion

Each degree (PhD, Bachelors, High School Diploma, and Elementary Education) is representative of how metaphorically educated the INTP is when exercising those personality traits.

INTROVERTED PERSONALITY TRAITS

EXTRAVERTED PERSONALITY TRAITS

PREDICTION

THEORIZING

BACHELORS DEGREE

PERCEIVING
PERSONALITY
TRAITS

CONSISTENCY

ADAPTABILITY

HIGH SCHOOL DIPLOMA

SOUL SEARCHING

COMPASSION

DECISION-MAKING
PERSONALITY
TRAITS

ELEMENTARY EDUCATION

PhD

VALIDITY

ORGANIZATION

The INTP PhD is in Introverted Thinking, and I have nicknamed it "Validity." With a PhD in Validity, the INTP is a metaphorical educational genius or expert when it comes to the personality trait of Validity.

They have a unique, introverted logic that seeks multiple ways of analyzing a problem. Validity is not concerned whether society thinks an idea is linearly logical. It is more concerned with non-linear logic. It is an ingenious logic that is able to break down concepts, theories, and ideas in ways that make sense to the INTP.

A good example of this is the terms megabyte and gigabyte. These words meant nothing fifty years ago. However, those with the Validity personality trait across the computer engineering industry decided those terms made sense to establish a storage system classification for computer data.

Their Bachelor's Degree is in Extraverted Intuition, but I have nicknamed it "Theorizing." With a Bachelor's Degree in Theorizing, they know a fair amount about how to utilize this personality trait—it also helps them have a more integrated personality that gets them engaged with the outside world. Again, what leads to the most personal development and growth for each Myers-Briggs type is further educating their Bachelor's Degree. INTPs have the intuitive ability to theorize about the external environment, ideas, and patterns they encounter daily to form unique thoughts and ideas. When mentally healthy, they love to explore new places, ideas, concepts, people, and emotions to develop their own personal theories on why things work the way they do.

A good example of this is the INTP, Albert Einstein. He had the ability to use his PhD in Validity to create theories that were then applied to the external world.

Their High School Diploma is in Introverted Sensing, but I nick-named it "Consistency." We default to this metaphorical degree under stress. Another way to perceive it is that we react with the emotional maturity of a high school student when the High School Diploma personality trait is being used. Therefore, the INTP reacts by not keeping their commitments and gives up on predictability in their daily lives. This personality trait is a weakness for the INTP, but the High School diploma of Consistency can be further educated through personal development and growth.

An example of this is ignoring daily chores when under stress.

Finally, the INTP Elementary Education is Extraverted Feeling, but I have nicknamed it "Compassion." The INTP uses this personality trait under severe stress. Their emotional maturity when using this personality trait is the metaphorical equivalent of an elementary school student. They typically feel awkward when they are put in a situation where they have to be sure everyone's emotional needs are met. They can come off as harsh, insensitive, or aloof when dealing with the feelings of those around them.

An example of this is an INTP becoming highly insensitive with their behavior in a group setting.

It's important to note that there are four more personality traits that are not part of the INTP personality. Each Myers-Briggs type only uses four of the eight personality traits. The four personality traits of Introverted Feeling - nickname: Soul Searching, Introverted Intuition - nickname: Prediction, Extraverted Sensing - nickname: Adaptability, and Extraverted Thinking - nickname: Organization are not on the INTP Education Model. This is because they are blind spots for the INTP and they do not exist in their personality trait stack. There is either massive resistance or an attempt at understanding when an INTP encounters those four personality traits that are blind spots in social interaction with another person. In other words, they are intrigued by their blind spots for better or for worse.

INTP Career Recommendations:

- **Architect**
- **Attorney**
- **Computer Engineer**
- **Musician**
- **Scientist**

Famous INTPs:

- **Albert Einstein**
- **Aubrey Plaza**
- **Bo Burnham**
- **Jordan Peterson**
- **Tina Fey**

2. ENTP

ENTP Education Model	
PhD	Theorizing
Bachelor's Degree	Validity
High School Diploma	Compassion
Elementary Education	Consistency

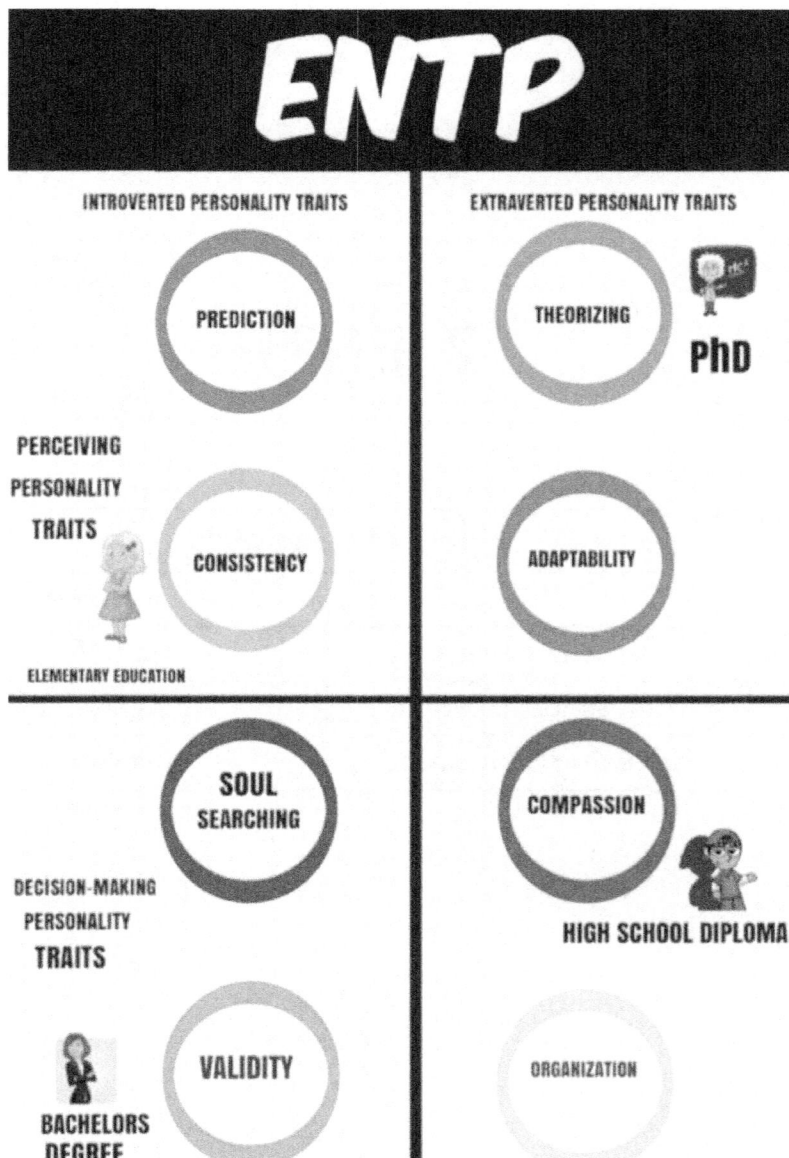

The ENTP PhD is in Extraverted Intuition, and I have nicknamed it "Theorizing." With a PhD in Theorizing, the ENTP is a metaphorical educational genius or expert when it comes to the personality trait of Theorizing.

With a PhD in Theorizing, they love to explore new places, ideas, concepts, people, and emotions to develop their own personal theories on why things work the way they do.

They have a unique, exploratory, and adventurous way of tying concepts together into a theory. This perceiving personality trait is intuitive; therefore, they may not be able to explain how they know what they know about the external world.

Some great examples of this are entrepreneurship and stand-up comedy. Again, ENTPS are able to pick up on patterns, ideas, and emotions in the external world that are a "blind spot" at an expert level compared to other personality types (excluding the ENFP). This perceived information they gather is then used to start a new business idea or have a unique stand-up comedy routine.

Their Bachelor's Degree is in Introverted Thinking, but I have nicknamed it "Validity." With a Bachelor's Degree in Validity, they know a fair amount about how to use this personality trait—it also helps them have a more integrated personality that gets them engaged in their inner world. Again, what leads to the most personal development and growth for each Myers-Briggs type is further educating their Bachelor's Degree personality trait. ENTPs have the ability to validate the patterns and ideas they perceive in their PhD of Theorizing. They have a unique, introverted logic that seeks multiple ways of analyzing a problem. Validity is not concerned whether society thinks an idea is logical. Again, it is a non-linear logic that experiments with different logical angles to a situation. It is an ingenious logic that can break down concepts, theories, and ideas in ways that make sense to the ENTP.

An example of this is attorneys. Statistically speaking, quite a few ENTPs are attorneys. They use their PhD of Theorizing and Bachelor's Degree in Validity to make a strong prosecution or defense case to uncover the truth. They are excellent debaters when their PhD and Bachelor's Degree personality traits are used in conjunction with one another and often. This is also often the reason they are nicknamed "The Devil's Advocate."

Their High School Diploma is in Extraverted Feeling, but I nicknamed it "Compassion." We default to this metaphorical degree under stress. Another way to perceive it is that we react with the emotional maturity of a high school student when the High School Diploma personality trait is being used. Therefore, the ENTP reacts by being very insensitive, scattered, and, sometimes, emotionally manipulative. This personality trait is a weakness for the ENTP, but the metaphorical High School Diploma can be further educated through personal development and growth. This would manifest in the ENTP being more patient, understanding, and compassionate towards others when they do not see the world as they do.

An example of this is ENTP and political commentator, Bill Maher, when he is in a heated political debate and his remarks become too offensive and personal.

Finally, the ENTP Elementary Education is Introverted Sensing, but I have nicknamed it "Consistency." The ENTP uses this personality trait under severe stress. It is called Elementary Education because this personality trait has the maturity of an elementary student. They feel as though they cannot stick to a consistent routine at times, and they are not one to stick to traditions. Under severe stress, the ENTP can become rebellious, egotistical, and flighty.

An example of this an ENTP moving from job to job once it has become monotonous in some way.

It's important to note that there are four more personality traits that are not part of the ENTP Personality. Each Myers-Briggs type only uses four of the eight cognitive personality traits. The four personality traits of Introverted Feeling - nickname: Soul Searching, Introverted Intuition - nickname: Prediction, Extraverted Sensing - nickname: Adaptability, and Extraverted Thinking - nickname: Organization are not on the ENTP Education Model. This is because they are blind spots for the ENTP and they do not exist in their personality trait stack. There is either massive resistance or an attempt at understanding when an ENTP encounters those four personality traits that are blind spots in social interaction with another person. In other words, they are intrigued by their blind spots for better or for worse.

ENTP Career Recommendations:

- **Attorney**
- **Entrepreneur**
- **Real Estate Agent**
- **Salesperson**
- **Stand Up Comedian**

Famous ENTPs:

- **Barack Obama**
- **Celine Dion**
- **Conan O'Brien**
- **Newt Gingrich**
- **Salma Hayek**

3. ENFJ

ENFJ Education Model	
PhD	Compassion
Bachelor's Degree	Prediction
High School Diploma	Adaptability
Elementary Education	Validity

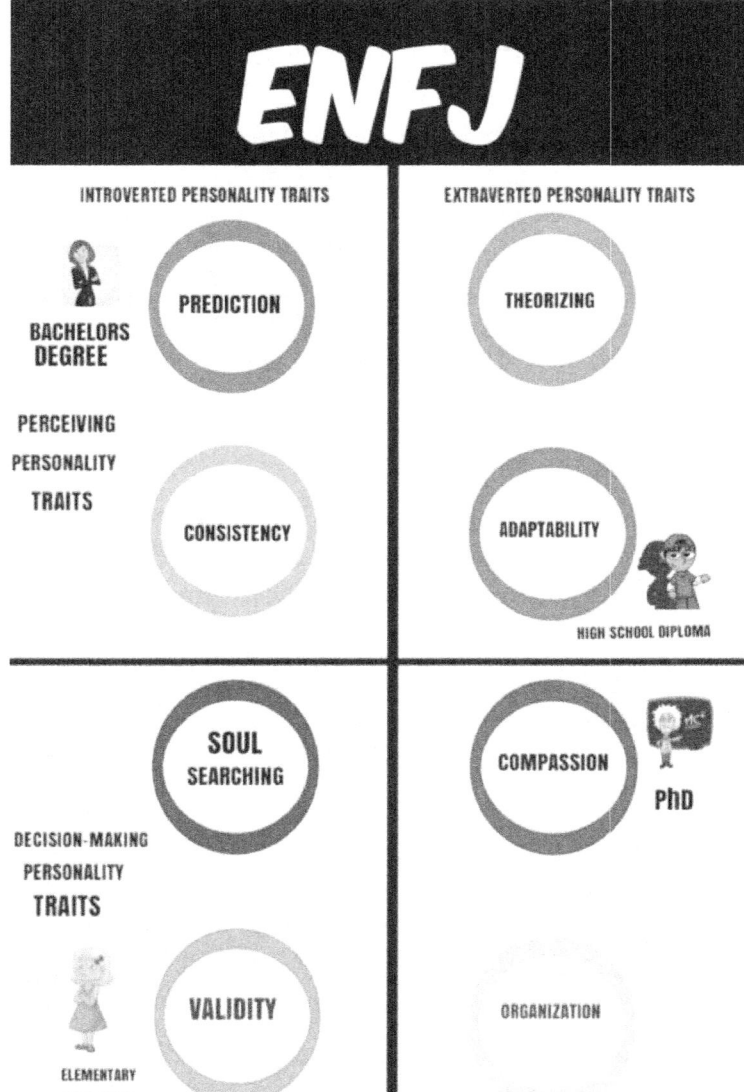

ENFJ

INTROVERTED PERSONALITY TRAITS

EXTRAVERTED PERSONALITY TRAITS

BACHELORS DEGREE

PREDICTION

THEORIZING

PERCEIVING PERSONALITY TRAITS

CONSISTENCY

ADAPTABILITY

HIGH SCHOOL DIPLOMA

SOUL SEARCHING

COMPASSION

PhD

DECISION-MAKING PERSONALITY TRAITS

VALIDITY

ORGANIZATION

ELEMENTARY EDUCATION

The ENFJ PhD is in Extraverted Feeling, and I have nicknamed it "Compassion." With a PhD in Compassion, the ENFJ is a metaphorical educational genius or expert when it comes to the personality trait of Compassion.

With a PhD in Compassion, they are caring and dutiful towards people's emotional needs. They are one of the two most helpful types in the Myers-Briggs personality system—with the other being the ESFJ.

ENFJs have explained that they have the uncanny ability to sense the feelings around them. This makes way for a type that has extremely high emotional intelligence.

Some great examples of this are a nurse or a politician who are very in tune with the feelings of their patients/constituents. They genuinely care that everyone around them has their needs met. This can also be illustrated when this type often takes charge of managing non-profit events and associations.

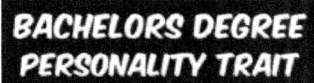

Their Bachelor's Degree is in Introverted Intuition, but I have nicknamed it "Prediction." With a Bachelor's Degree in Prediction, they know a fair amount about how to utilize this personality trait—it also helps them have a more integrated personality that gets them engaged in their inner world. Again, what leads to the most personal development and growth for each Myers-Briggs type is further educating their Bachelor's Degree personality trait. ENFJs have the intuitive ability to find the best approach to doing something. They have an uncanny talent of being able to put themselves in "other people's shoes." They then use this intuitive knowledge as a "road map" for how to handle various situations. It is a personality trait that can look into the future and predict what will be. This, in conjunction with the Compassion personality trait, creates an innovative manager of others feelings.

An example of this is a hospital administrator who has to constantly think about how to manage the feelings of doctors and nurses. They have to be innovative, charismatic, and compassionate toward employees/contractors that have to care for others in life-threatening situations professionally in order to save lives.

Their High School Diploma is in Extraverted Sensing, but I nick-named it "Adaptability." We default to this metaphorical degree under stress. Another way to perceive it is that we react with the emotional maturity of a high school student when the High School Diploma personality trait is being used. Therefore, the ENFJ reacts by being extremely resistant to change, stubborn, and prone to substance abuse. This personality trait is a weakness for the ENFJ, but the metaphorical High School Diploma can be fur-ther educated through personal development and growth. This would manifest in the ENFJ being more introspective and reflect-ive toward changes in their lives. They can also put their needs above others to escape this personality trait.

Finally, the ENFJ Elementary Education is in Introverted Thinking, but I nicknamed it "Validity." We default to this metaphorical degree under severe stress. Another way to perceive it is that we react with the emotional maturity of an elementary school student when the Elementary Education personality trait is being used. Therefore, the ENFJ reacts by being very divergent in their thinking, scattered, and, sometimes, emotionally manipulative toward others. At times, they may even appear obsessive-compulsive in their personal and professional lives.

This personality trait is a weakness for the ENFJ, but the metaphorical Elementary Education can be further educated through personal development and growth. This would manifest in the ENFJ being more level-headed, "slowing down," and reflective towards others when they do not see the world as they do.

It's important to note that there are four more personality traits that are not part of the ENFJ Personality. Each Myers-Briggs type only uses four of the eight personality traits. The four personality traits of Introverted Feeling - nickname: Soul Searching, Extraverted Intuition - nickname: Theorizing, Introverted Sensing - nickname: Consistency, and Extraverted Thinking - nickname: Organization are not on the ENFJ Education Model. This is because they are blind spots for the ENFJ and they do not exist in their personality trait stack. There is either massive resistance or an attempt at understanding when an ENFJ encounters those four personality traits that are blind spots in social interaction with another person. In other words, they are intrigued by their blind spots for better or for worse.

ENFJ Career Recommendations:

- **Actor**
- **Human Resources Manager**
- **Politician**
- **Salesperson**
- **Teacher**

Famous ENFJs:

- **Alexandria Ocasio-Cortez**
- **Joe Biden**
- **Morgan Freeman**
- **Oprah**
- **Ronald Reagan**

4. INFJ

INFJ Education Model	
PhD	Prediction
Bachelor's Degree	Compassion
High School Diploma	Validity
Elementary Education	Adaptability

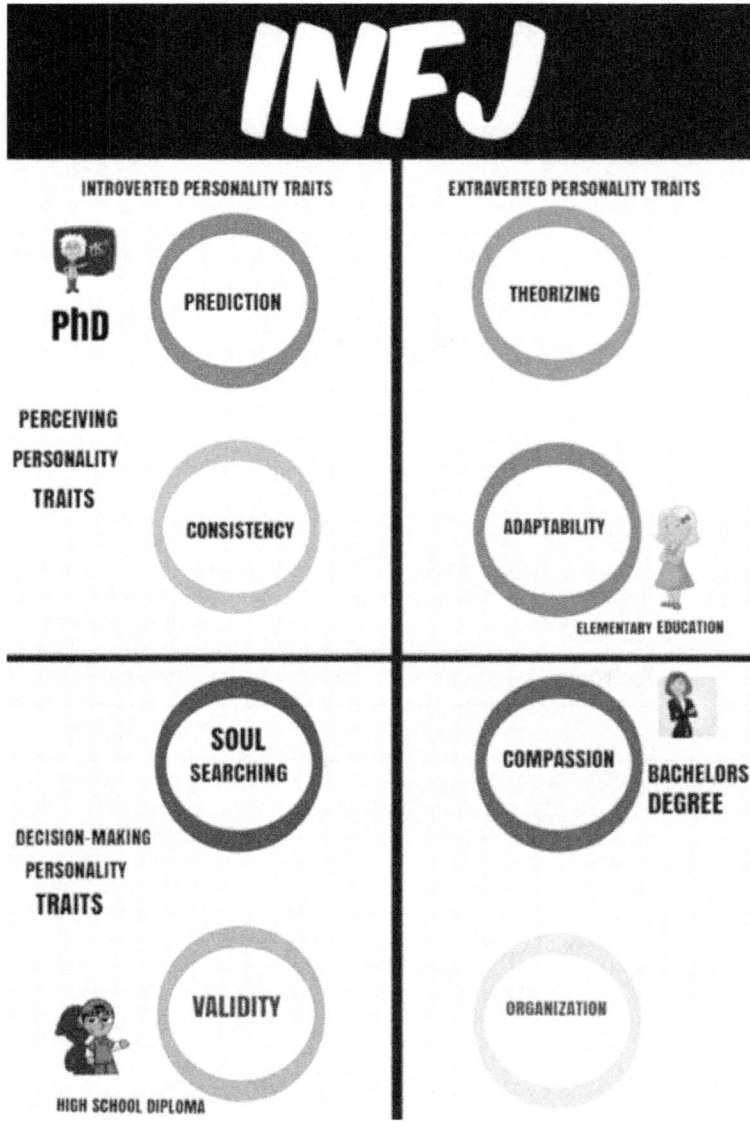

The INFJ PhD is in Introverted Intuition, and I have nicknamed it "Prediction." With a PhD in Prediction, the INFJ is a metaphorical educational genius or expert when it comes to the personality trait of Prediction.

With a PhD in Prediction, INFJs have the intuitive ability to find the best approach to doing something. They have an uncanny talent to be able to put themselves in "other people's shoes." They then use this intuitive knowledge as a "road map" for how to handle various situations.

An example of this is a clinical mental health counselor. Great counselors are able to empathize with their clients and uncover the patterns that are perpetually being destructive to the client's life. INFJs are able to develop the best approach to alleviating their pain.

Their Bachelor's Degree is in Extraverted Feeling, but I have nick-named it "Compassion." With a Bachelor's Degree in Compassion, they know a fair amount about how to utilize this personality trait —it also helps them have a more integrated personality that gets them engaged in the outer world. Again, what leads to the most personal development and growth for each Myers-Briggs type is further educating their Bachelor's Degree personality trait. They are caring and dutiful towards people's emotional needs. They are one of the most helpful types in the Myers-Briggs personality system.

INFJs have explained that they have the uncanny ability to sense the feelings around them." This makes way for a type that has extremely high emotional intelligence.

An example of this is a church pastor. An INFJ pastor can intuitively come up with the best solution to a problem by seeing things from another person's perspective. In conjunction with Compassion, they can counsel members of their congregation to the best solution while proposing strategies on how to deal with their emotions.

Their High School Diploma is in Extraverted Sensing, but I nicknamed it "Adaptability." We default to this metaphorical degree under stress. Another way to perceive it is that we react with the emotional maturity of a high school student when the High School Diploma personality trait is being used. Therefore, the INFJ reacts by being very divergent in their thinking, scattered, and, sometimes, self-obsessed. At times, they may even appear obsessive-compulsive in their personal and professional lives.

This personality trait is a weakness for the INFJ, but the metaphorical High School diploma can be further educated through personal development and growth. This would manifest in the INFJ being more in tune with other people's feelings, accepting the various outcomes in life, and seeking advice from friends and family to temporarily escape from their "inner world" of worry.

An example of this is a nurse being hard on themselves for not being able to save a patient's life even though they did everything they could.

Finally, the INFJ elementary Education is in Extraverted Sensing, but I nicknamed it "Adaptability." We default to this metaphorical degree under severe stress. Another way to perceive it is that we react with the emotional maturity of an elementary school student when the Elementary Education personality trait is being used. Therefore, the INFJ reacts by being very sensitive to their external environment. They often have trouble dealing with the unpleasant, necessary sounds of everyday life. They can also have a hard time getting comfortable in settings that are foreign to them. This personality trait is a weakness for the INFJ, but the metaphorical Elementary Education can be further educated through personal development and growth. This would look like the INFJ being more open to their external environment. Physical activities where you can be mindful of your external senses have been theorized to help with this.

An example of this is an INFJ being very sensitive to the loud noises at a restaurant while having a meal.

It's important to note that there are four more personality traits that are not part of the INFJ Personality. Each Myers-Briggs type only uses four of the eight. The personality traits of Introverted Feeling - nickname: Soul Searching, Extraverted Intuition - nickname: Theorizing, Introverted Sensing - nickname: Consistency, and Extraverted Thinking - nickname: Organization are not on the INFJ Model. This is because they are blind spots for the INFJ and they do not exist in their personality trait stack. There is either massive resistance or an attempt at understanding when an INFJ encounters those four personality traits that are blind spots in social interaction with another person. In other words, they are intrigued by their blind spots for better or for worse.

INFJ Career Recommendations:

- **Actor**
- **Artist and/or Musician**
- **Doctor**
- **Pastor**
- **Psychologist/ Counselor**

Famous INFJs:

- **Carl Jung**
- **Emma Watson**
- **Jesus**
- **Mother Theresa**
- **Nelson Mandela**

5. ENFP

ENFP Education Model	
PhD	Theorizing
Bachelor's Degree	Soul Searching
High School Diploma	Organization
Elementary Education	Consistency

ENFP

INTRODUCED PERSONALITY TRAITS

EXTRAVERTED PERSONALITY TRAITS

PREDICTION

THEORIZING

PERCEIVING
PERSONALITY
TRAITS

CONSISTENCY

ADAPTABILITY

ELEMENTARY EDUCATION

SOUL
SEARCHING

COMPASSION

DECISION-MAKING
PERSONALITY
TRAITS

BACHELORS DEGREE

HIGH SCHOOL DIPLOMA

VALIDITY

ORGANIZATION

PHD PERSONALITY TRAIT

The ENFP PhD is in Extraverted Intuition, and I have nicknamed it "Theorizing." With a PhD in Theorizing, the ENFP is a metaphorical educational genius or expert regarding the personality trait of Theorizing.

With a PhD in Theorizing, they love to explore new places, ideas, concepts, people, and emotions to develop their own personal theories on why things work the way they do.

They have a unique, exploratory, and adventurous way of tying concepts together into a theory. This perceiving personality trait is intuitive; therefore, they may not be able to explain their knowledge of the external world.

Some good examples of this are entrepreneurship and improvisational comedy. Again, ENFPS are able to pick up on patterns, ideas, and emotions in the external world that are a "blind spot" for the other personality types (other than the ENTP). This perceived information they gather is then used to start a new business idea or an improvisational comedy troupe.

Their Bachelor's Degree is in Introverted Feeling, but I have nicknamed it "Soul Searching." With a Bachelor's Degree in Soul Searching, they know a fair amount about how to utilize this personality trait—it also helps them have a more integrated personality that gets them engaged in their inner world. Again, what leads to the most personal development and growth for each Myers-Briggs type is further educating their Bachelor's Degree personality trait. ENFPs have the ability to validate the emotional patterns and ideas they perceive in their PhD of Theorizing. ENFPs have the unique talent of taking their creative insights they pick up in their external world and can put these insights into their own empathetic, personal value system.

ENFPs can develop this personality trait by "slowing down" and getting in touch with their "inner world" about whether to make a certain decision. They have to evaluate their bigger decisions in life with authenticity regarding their identities.

An example of this is actors/actresses. Actors are able to draw patterns, insights, and intuition from observing all the different lifestyles in the world. In conjunction with soul searching, they are able to "search their souls" to find the emotions and values as to why a person chooses a particular lifestyle.

Their High School Diploma is in Extraverted Thinking, but I nicknamed it "Organization." We default to this metaphorical degree under stress. Another way to perceive it is that we react with the emotional maturity of a high school student when the High School Diploma personality trait is being used. Therefore, the ENFP reacts by being very scattered, impulsive, anxious, and, sometimes, disorganized. This personality trait is a weakness for the ENFP, but the metaphorical High School diploma can be further educated through personal development and growth. This would manifest in the ENFP "slowing down," investigating different options when making life decisions, and not jumping to the most straightforward solution under stress.

Finally, the ENFP Elementary Education is Consistency, but I have nicknamed it "Consistency." The ENFP uses this personality trait under severe stress. They feel as though they cannot stick to a consistent routine at times, and they are not one to stick to traditions. Under severe stress, the ENFP can become rebellious, egotistical, and flighty.

An example of this is an ENFP feeling as though they are going to be stuck in a particular life situation "forever" even though that is simply and logically not true.

It's important to note that there are four more personality traits that are not part of the ENFP Personality. Each Myers-Briggs type only uses four of the eight personality traits. The four personality traits of Extraverted Feeling - nickname: Compassion, Introverted Intuition - nickname: Prediction, Extraverted Sensing - nickname: Adaptability, and Introverted Thinking - nickname: Validity are not on the ENFP Education Model. This is because they are blind spots for the ENFP and they do not exist in their personality trait stack. There is either massive resistance or an attempt at understanding when an ENFP encounters those four personality traits that are blind spots in social interaction with another person. In other words, they are intrigued by their blind spots for better or for worse.

ENFP Career Recommendations:

- **Actor**
- **Comedian**
- **Entrepreneur**
- **Psychologist/ Counselor**
- **Teacher**

Famous ENFPs:

- **Dave Chappelle**
- **Jennifer Anniston**
- **Jim Carrey**
- **Robin Williams**
- **Walt Disney**

6. INFP

INFP Education Model	
PhD	Soul Searching
Bachelor's Degree	Theorizing
High School Diploma	Consistency
Elementary Education	Organization

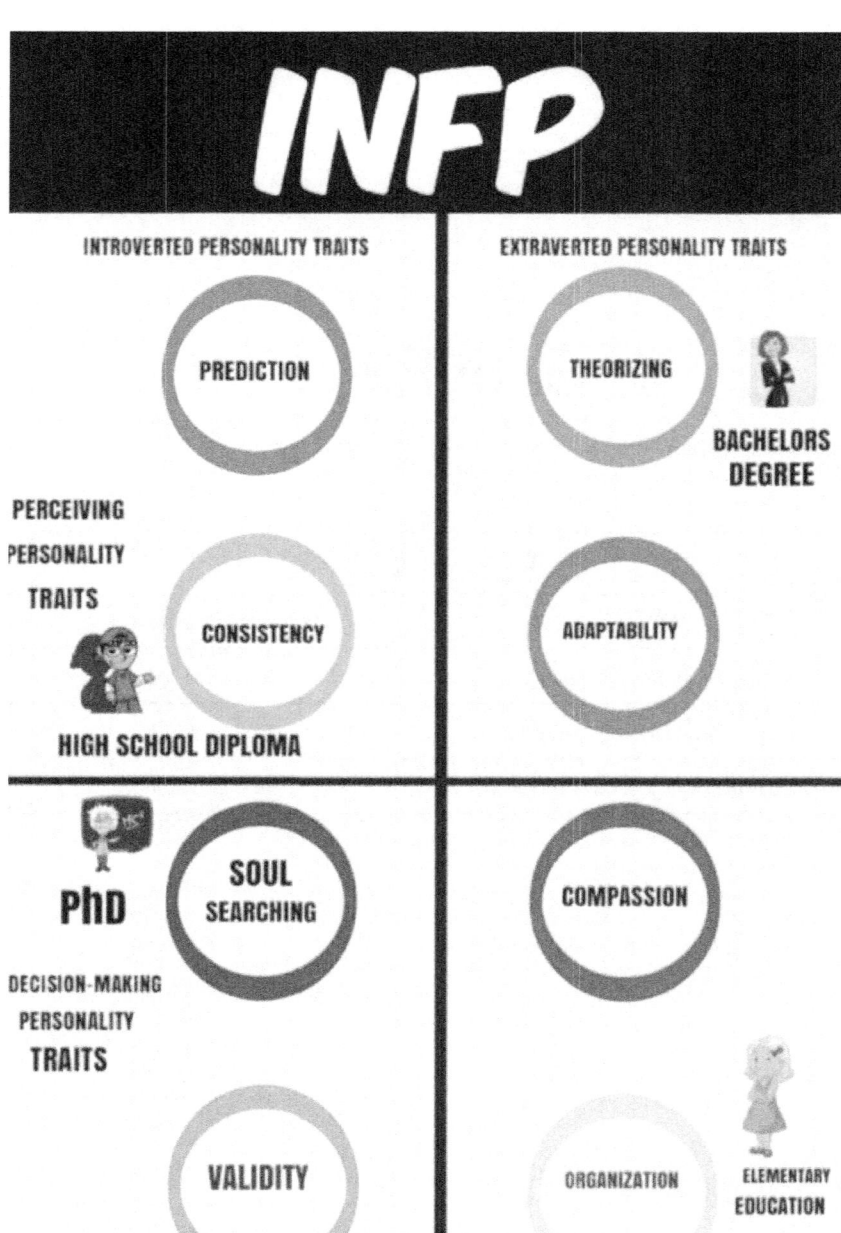

The INFP PhD is in Introverted Feeling, and I have nicknamed it "Soul Searching." With a PhD in Soul Searching, the INFP is a metaphorical educational genius or expert concerning the personality trait of Soul Searching.

With a PhD in Soul Searching, INFPs have the unique talent of being able to understand the emotions of others by being deeply introspective about their values and beliefs. They have an inherent gift of knowing what's "right" and "wrong." They are dreamers who stand up for their value of humanity.

An example of this is a writer who is able to write down the deepest and happiest parts of his or her mind in an effort to connect emotionally with the reader.

Their Bachelor's Degree is in Extraverted Intuition, but I have nicknamed it "Theorizing." With a Bachelor's Degree in Theorizing, they know a fair amount about how to utilize this personality trait—it also helps them have a more integrated personality that gets them engaged in their outer world. Again, what leads to the most personal development and growth for each Myers-Briggs type is further educating their Bachelor's Degree personality trait. With a Bachelor's Degree in Theorizing, they love to explore new places, ideas, concepts, people, and emotions to develop their own personal theories on why things work the way they do.

They have a unique, exploratory, and adventurous way of tying concepts together into a theory. This perceiving personality trait is intuitive; therefore, they may not be able to explain their knowledge about the external world.

An example of this is a fiction writer. INFPs are able to be authentic, honest, and value-driven. They take that foundation and use their Theorizing to write an elaborate fictional story with characters of all different emotions.

Their High School Diploma is in Introverted Sensing, but I nicknamed it "Consistency." We default to this metaphorical degree under stress. Another way to perceive it is that we react with the emotional maturity of a high school student when the High

School Diploma personality trait is being used. Therefore, the INFP reacts by not keeping their commitments and gets annoyed by the predictability in their daily lives. This personality trait is a weakness for the INFP, but it can be the metaphorical High School Diploma if Consistency can be further educated through personal development and growth.

An example of this is moving from one creative project to another once the "newness" of it wears off.

Finally, the INFP Elementary Education is Extraverted Thinking, but I nicknamed it "Organization." We default to this metaphorical degree under severe stress. Another way to perceive it is that we react with the emotional maturity of a high school student when the High School Diploma personality trait is being used. Therefore, the INFP reacts by being very scattered, anxious, impulsive, and, sometimes, disorganized. This personality trait is a weakness for the INFP, but the metaphorical Elementary Education can be further educated through personal development and growth. This would manifest in the INFP investigating different mentor options when making life decisions, not jumping to the most straightforward solution under stress, and realizing they should focus on one idea at a time. Networking their ideas can be hard at first, but once they do it, they can put some of the most imaginative ideas into action.

It's important to note that there are four more personality traits that are not part of the INFP personality. Each Myers-Briggs type only uses four of the eight personality traits. The four personality traits of Extraverted Feeling - nickname: Compassion, Introverted Intuition - nickname: Prediction, Extraverted Sensing - nickname: Adaptability, and Introverted Thinking - nickname: Validity are not on the INFP Education Model. This is because they are blind spots for the INFP and they do not exist in their personality trait stack. There is either massive resistance or an attempt at understanding when an INFP encounters those four personality traits that are blind spots in social interaction with another person. In other words, they are intrigued by their blind spots for better or for worse.

INFP Career Recommendations:

- **Actor**
- **Artist**
- **Author**
- **Musician**
- **Pastor**

Famous INFPs:

- **Halsey**
- **J.K. Rowling**
- **Lana Del Rey**
- **Stephen Colbert**
- **Vincent Van Gogh**

7. ENTJ

ENTJ Education Model	
PhD	Organization
Bachelor's Degree	Prediction
High School Diploma	Adaptability
Elementary Education	Soul Searching

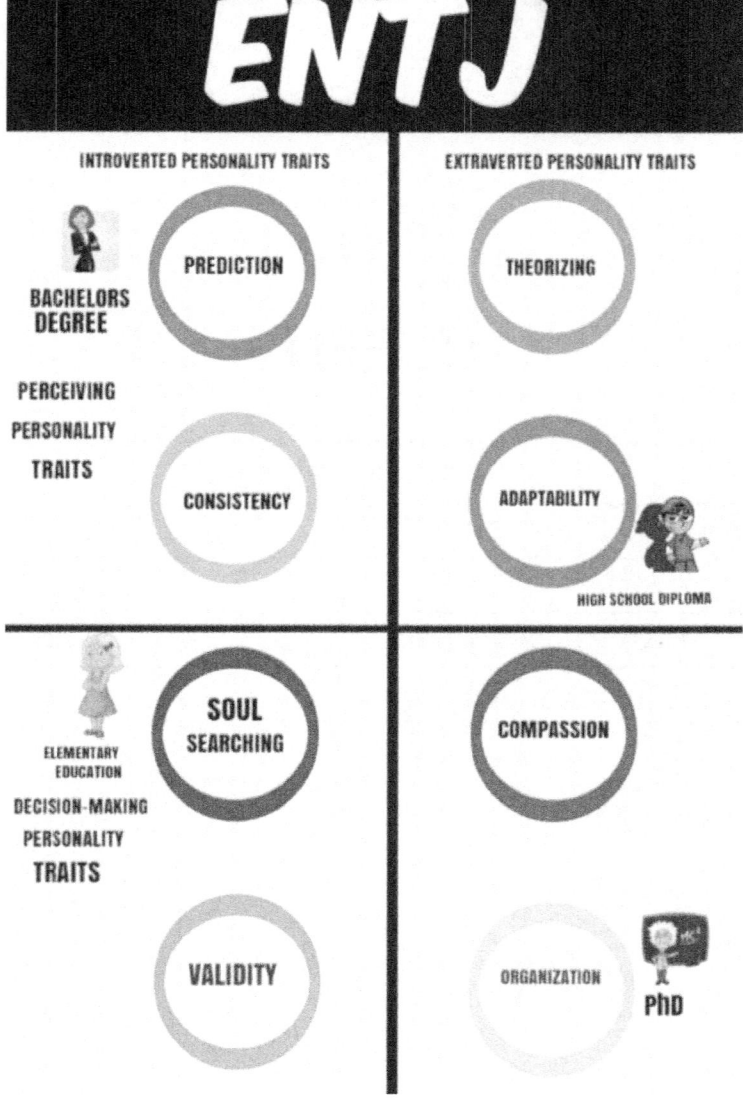

PHD PERSONALITY TRAIT

The ENTJ PhD is in Extraverted Thinking, and I have nicknamed it "Organization." With a PhD in Organization, the ENTJ is a metaphorical educational genius or expert when it comes to the personality trait of Organization.

With a PhD in Organization, they are managerial, effective, and efficient towards people's logistical needs.

ENTJs have the ability to bring order to chaos. They are logical and steadfast under pressure, and they come up with the most effective solution to problems for people and things when dealing with logistical matters.

A good example of this is a CEO that is very effective and efficient at understanding where the business needs improvement. They are able to think logistically "on their feet."

Their Bachelor's Degree is in Introverted Intuition, but I have nicknamed it "Prediction." With a Bachelor's Degree in Prediction, they know a fair amount about how to utilize this personality trait – it also helps them have a more integrated personality that gets them engaged in their inner world. Again, what leads to the most personal development and growth for each Myers-Briggs type is further educating their Bachelor's Degree personality trait. ENTJs have the intuitive ability to find the best approach to doing something. They have an uncanny talent to be able to put themselves in "other people's shoes." They then use this intuitive knowledge as a "road map" for how to handle various managerial situations in their life. It is a personality trait that can look into the future to determine what will become of a particular situation. This, in conjunction with the PhD in Organization personality trait, creates an innovative manager of people's behaviors.

An example of this is a stock market investor who has to constantly think about how to put themselves in the metaphorical shoes of a CEO of any given company. They have to be careful, analytical, and thoughtful when choosing a company stock to purchase. They can use their PhD and Bachelor's Degree to make insightful stock picks that they intuitively feel are the best option after reading about a company's numbers almost as if they were CEO of that company.

Their High School Diploma is in Extraverted Sensing, but I nicknamed it "Adaptability." We default to this metaphorical degree under stress. Another way to perceive it is that we react with the emotional maturity of a high school student when the High School Diploma personality trait is being used. Therefore, the ENTJ reacts by being extremely resistant to change, stubborn, and prone to substance abuse. This personality trait is a weakness for the ENTJ, but the metaphorical High School diploma can be further educated through personal development and growth. This would manifest in the ENTJ being more introspective and reflective toward changes in their lives. They also can put other people's needs above their own to help escape this stress cycle.

An example of this is turning to an addictive, unhealthy habit when under stress.

Finally, the ENTJ Elementary Education is in Introverted Feeling, but I nicknamed it "Soul Searching." We default to this metaphorical degree under severe stress. Another way to perceive it is that we react with the emotional maturity of an elementary school student when the Elementary Education personality trait is being used. Therefore, the ENTJ reacts by being severely judgmental, angry, and not open to being vulnerable.

An example of this is an executive not being willing to admit he or she made a mistake.

This personality trait is a weakness for the ENTJ, but the metaphorical Elementary Education can be further educated through personal development and growth. This would manifest in the ENTJ "slowing down," using logical criticism instead of personal criticism, and being vulnerable to other people who can provide emotional support. ENTJs have a tendency to insist they do not need emotional support even though everyone does.

It's important to note that there are four more personality traits that are not part of the ENTJ personality. Each Myers-Briggs type only uses four of the eight personality traits. The four personality traits of Extraverted Feeling - nickname: Compassion, Extraverted

Intuition - nickname: Theorizing, Introverted Sensing - nickname: Consistency, and Introverted Thinking - nickname: Validity are not on the ENTJ Education Model. This is because they are blind spots for the ENTJ and they do not exist in their personality trait stack. There is either massive resistance or an attempt at understanding when an ENTJ encounters those four personality traits that are blind spots in social interaction with another person. In other words, they are intrigued by their blind spots for better or for worse.

ENTJ Career Recommendations:

- **Business Executive**
- **Financial Analyst**
- **Politician**
- **Sales Manager**
- **Software Developer**

Famous ENTJs:

- **Adele**
- **Bill Gates**
- **Franklin D. Roosevelt**
- **Margaret Thatcher**
- **Steve Jobs**

8. INTJ

INTJ Education Model	
PhD	Prediction
Bachelor's Degree	Organization
High School Diploma	Soul Searching
Elementary Education	Adaptability

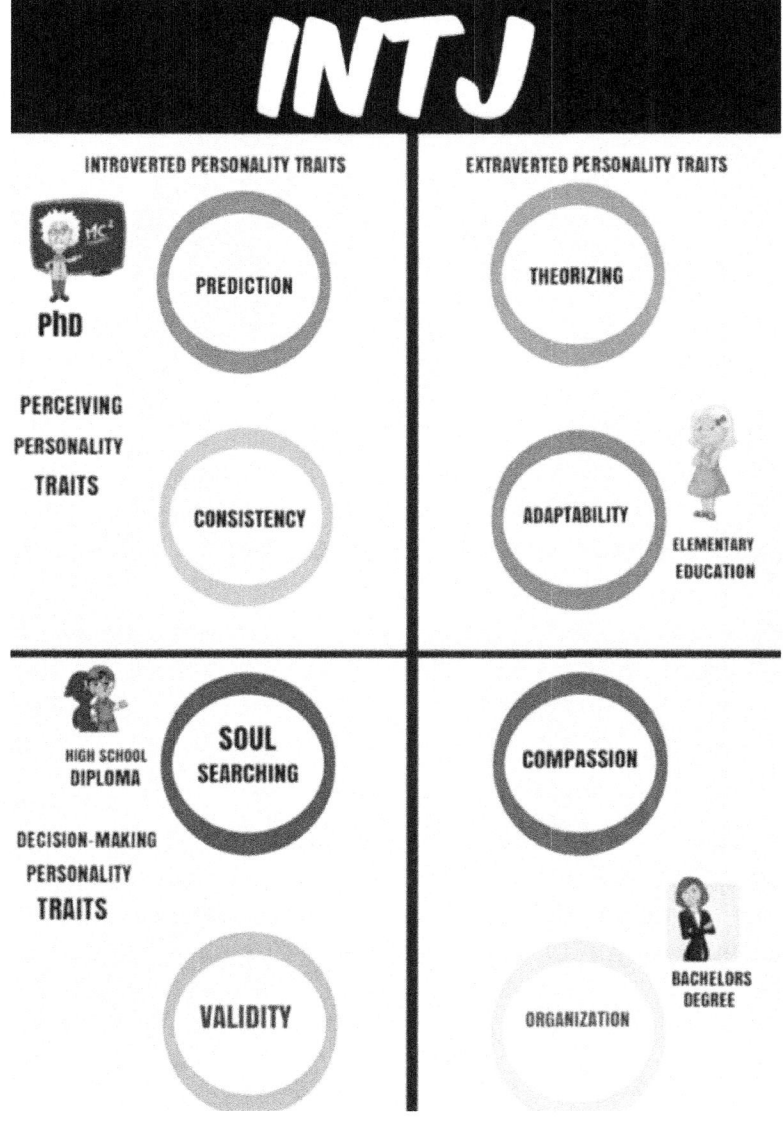

The INTJ PhD is in Introverted Intuition, and I have nicknamed it "Prediction." With a PhD in Prediction, the INTJ is a metaphorical educational genius or expert regarding the personality trait of Prediction.

With a PhD in Prediction, INTJs have the intuitive ability to find the best approach to doing something. They have an uncanny talent to be able to put themselves in "other people's shoes." They then use this intuitive knowledge as a "road map" for how to handle various situations.

A good example of this is a board member of a company. An INTJ can use their Prediction to forecast the earnings for the next quarter from an intuitive standpoint. It is their gift to be able to determine "what will happen" from a logistical perspective.

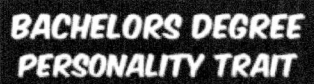

The INTJ Bachelor's Degree is in Extraverted Thinking, and I have nicknamed it "Organization." With a Bachelor's Degree in Organization, they know a fair amount about how to utilize this personality trait – it also helps them have a more integrated personality that gets them engaged in their inner world. Again, what leads to the most personal development and growth for each Myers-Briggs type is further educating their Bachelor's Degree personality trait. With a Bachelor's Degree in Organization, they are managerial, effective, and efficient towards people's logistical needs.

INTJs have the ability to bring order to chaos. They are logical and steadfast under pressure, and they come up with the most effective solution to problems for people and things when dealing with logistical matters. This, in conjunction with prediction, makes way for a visionary, analytical, futuristic, and intelligent type.

A good example of this is an INTJ CEO, Elon Musk. Musk is clearly able to gather logistical, intuitive data on outer space for planning launches and construction. He is able to take his interest in the unknown of space exploration and apply logical management steps to accomplish his organization's goals.

Their High School Diploma is in Introverted Feeling, but I nicknamed it "Soul Searching." We default to this metaphorical degree under stress. Another way to perceive it is that we react with the emotional maturity of a high school student when the High School Diploma personality trait is being used. Therefore, the INTJ reacts by being severely judgmental, angry, and not open to being vulnerable.

An example of this is an INTJ judging someone else for choosing to live a lifestyle that is different from their own.

This personality trait is a weakness for the INTJ, but the metaphorical High School Diploma can be further educated through personal development and growth. This would manifest in the INTJ "slowing down," using logistical criticism instead of personal criticism, and being vulnerable to other people who can provide emotional support. INTJs have a tendency to insist they do not need emotional support even though everyone does.

Finally, the INTJ Elementary Education is in Extraverted Sensing, but I nicknamed it "Adaptability." We default to this metaphorical degree under severe stress. Another way to perceive it is that we react with the emotional maturity of an elementary school student when the Elementary Education personality trait is being used. Therefore, the INTJ reacts by being very sensitive to their external environment. They often have trouble dealing with the unpleasant, necessary sounds of everyday life. They can also have a hard time getting comfortable in settings that are foreign to them. This personality trait is a weakness for the INTJ, but the metaphorical Elementary Education can be further educated through personal development and growth. This would manifest in the INTJ being more open to their external environment. Physical activities where you can be mindful of your external senses have been theorized to help with this.

An example of this is an INTJ enjoying the taste of a certain food but not the texture.

It's important to note that there are four more personality traits that are not part of the INTJ Personality. Each Myers-Briggs type only uses four of the eight personality traits. The four personality traits of Extraverted Feeling - nickname: Compassion, Extraverted Intuition - nickname: Theorizing, Introverted Sensing - nickname: Consistency, and Introverted Thinking - nickname: Validity are not on the INTJ Education Model. This is because they are blind spots for the INTJ and they do not exist in their personality trait stack. There is either massive resistance or an attempt at understanding when an INTJ encounters those four personality traits that are blind spots in social interaction with another person. In other words, they are intrigued by their blind spots for better or for worse.

INTJ Career Recommendations:

- **Business Executive**
- **Engineer**
- **Entrepreneur**
- **Musician**
- **Scientist**

Famous INTJs:

- **Annie Clark(St. Vincent)**
- **Elon Musk**
- **Jane Austen**
- **Mark Zuckerberg**
- **Vladimir Putin**

9. ESTP

ESTP Education Model	
PhD	Adaptability
Bachelor's Degree	Validity
High School Diploma	Compassion
Elementary Education	Prediction

INTROVERTED PERSONALITY TRAITS

EXTRAVERTED PERSONALITY TRAITS

ELEMENTARY
EDUCATION

PREDICTION

THEORIZING

**PERCEIVING
PERSONALITY
TRAITS**

CONSISTENCY

ADAPTABILITY

PhD

SOUL
SEARCHING

COMPASSION

**DECISION-MAKING
PERSONALITY
TRAITS**

HIGH SCHOOL DIPLOMA

**BACHELORS
DEGREE**

VALIDITY

ORGANIZATION

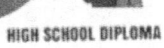

The ESTP PhD is in Extraverted Sensing, and I have nicknamed it "Adaptability." With a PhD in Adaptability, the ESTP is a metaphorical educational genius or expert concerning the personality trait of Adaptability.

With a PhD in Adaptability, they love to improvise with their external senses. This includes sight, sound, touch, smell, and taste. They love using this expert awareness of these senses to try new things, be spontaneous, and seek thrills.

They have an ongoing memory of how their external senses reacted in particular situations.

Some good examples of this are riding motorcycles, improvising in a speech, or working with their hands.

Their Bachelor's Degree is in Introverted Thinking, but I have nicknamed it "Validity." With a Bachelor's Degree in Validity, they know a fair amount about how to utilize this personality trait— it also helps them have a more integrated personality that gets them engaged in their inner world. Again, what leads to the most personal development and growth for each Myers-Briggs type is further educating their Bachelor's Degree personality trait. ESTPs have the ability to validate their external senses to acquire knowledge and experience. They have a unique, introverted logic that seeks multiple ways of analyzing a problem. Validity is not concerned whether society thinks an idea is logical. It is an ingenious logic that is able to break down concepts, theories, and ideas in ways that make sense to the Validity user.

An example of this is business owners. Statistically speaking, quite a few ESTPs are business owners. They use their PhD of Adaptability and Bachelors Degree of Validity to come up with ideas that relieve the external senses for the rest of us. In other words, they are good at starting businesses that solve a "pain" in everyday life.

Their High School Diploma is in Extraverted Feeling, but I nick-named it "Compassion." We default to this metaphorical degree under stress. Another way to perceive it is that we react with the emotional maturity of a high school student when the High School Diploma personality trait is being used. Therefore, the ESTP reacts by being insensitive, scattered, and, sometimes, emotionally manipulative. This personality trait is a weakness for the ESTP, but the metaphorical High School diploma can be further educated through personal development and growth. This would manifest in the ESTP being more patient, understanding, and compassionate towards others when they do not see the world as they do.

An example of this would be President Donald Trump "lashing out" at someone in public because they do not see the world the same way he does.

Finally, the ESTP Elementary Education is Introverted Intuition, but I have nicknamed it "Prediction." The ESTP uses this personality trait under severe stress. When this occurs, ESTPs insist that tasks are much easier to accomplish than they actually are. They spring into action without thinking about the consequences of those actions. They can become very hard-headed, foolish, and belligerent when in this state.

An example of this is an ESTP putting water in their vehicle radiator and thinking "it should be fine for a while."

It's important to note that there are four more personality traits that are not part of the ESTP Personality. Each Myers-Briggs type only uses four of the eight personality traits. The four personality traits of Introverted Feeling - nickname: Soul Searching, Extraverted Intuition - nickname: Theorizing, Introverted Sensing - nickname: Consistency, and Extraverted Thinking - nickname: Organization are not on the ESTP Education Model. This is because they are blind spots for the ESTP and they do not exist in their personality trait stack. There is either massive resistance or an attempt at understanding when an ESTP encounters those four personality traits that are blind spots in social interaction with another person. In other words, they are intrigued by their blind spots for better or for worse. **ESTP Career Recommendations:**

- **Athlete**
- **Business Owner**
- **Comedian**
- **Real Estate Developer**
- **Salesperson**

Famous ESTPs:

- **Angelina Jolie**
- **Charlie Sheen**
- **Donald Trump**
- **Joe Rogan**
- **Madonna**

10. ISTP

ISTP Education Model	
PhD	Validity
Bachelor's Degree	Adaptability
High School Diploma	Prediction
Elementary Education	Compassion

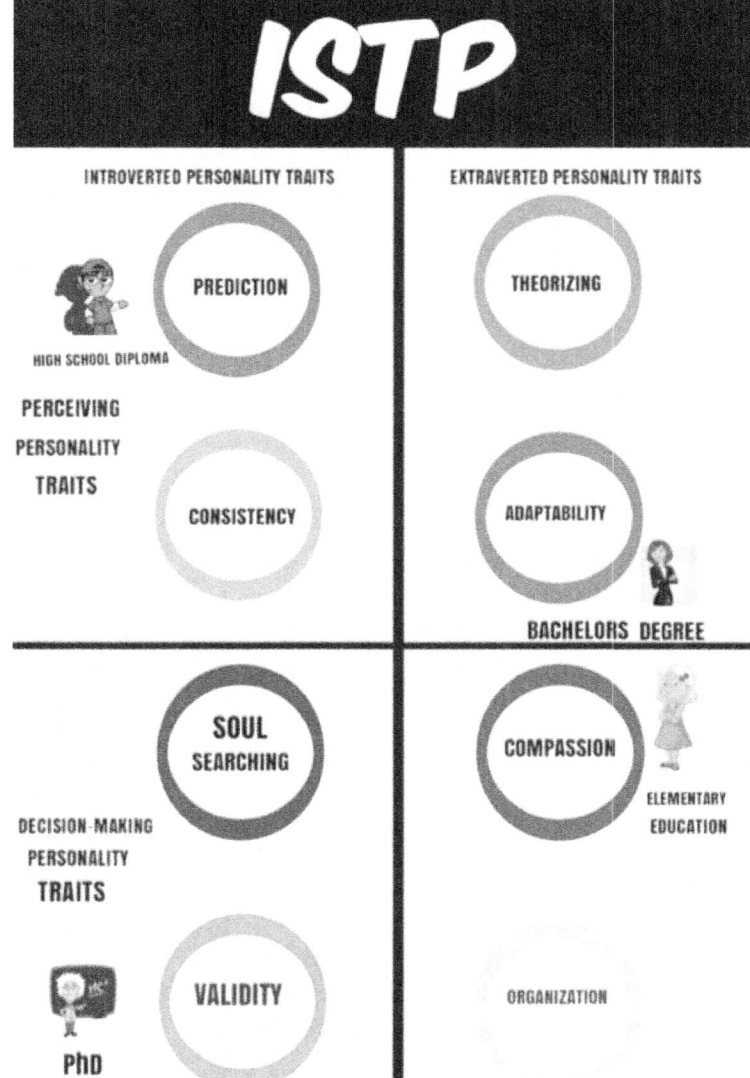

The ISTP PhD is in Introverted Thinking, and I have nicknamed it "Validity." With a PhD in Validity, the ISTP is a metaphorical educational genius or expert concerning the personality trait of Validity.

They have a unique, introverted logic that seeks multiple ways of analyzing a problem. Validity is not concerned whether society thinks an idea is logical. It is an ingenious and non-linear logic that is able to break down concepts, theories, and ideas in ways that make sense to the Validity user.

A good example of this are the YouTube videos of men and women coming up with unique ways of fixing or assembling parts that are mechanical, electrical, etc.

Their Bachelor's Degree is in Extraverted Sensing, but I have nicknamed it "Adaptability." With a Bachelor's Degree in Adaptability, they know a fair amount about how to utilize this personality trait—it also helps them have a more integrated personality that gets them engaged with the outside world. Again, what leads to the most personal development and growth for each Myers-Briggs type is further educating their Bachelor's Degree. ISTPs love to improvise with their external senses. This includes sight, sound, touch, smell, and taste. They love using this expert awareness of their senses to try new things, be spontaneous, and seek thrills.

They have an ongoing memory of how their external senses reacted in particular situations.

A good example of this is when they use their Validity and Adaptability in conjunction with one another to create situations in which they can fix various things with their hands, assembling construction models, architecture, etc. They also like to use this ability to come up with adventurous ideas for seeking a thrill.

Their High School Diploma is in Introverted Sensing, but I nicknamed it "Consistency." We default to this metaphorical degree under stress. Another way to perceive it is that we react with the emotional maturity of a high school student when the High School Diploma personality trait is being used. When this occurs, ISTPs insist that tasks are much easier to accomplish than they actually are. They spring into action without thinking about the consequences of those actions. They can become impulsive, overly focused on manual tasks as a form of escaping, and sometimes, angry/belligerent when in this state.

An example of this is repeating the same mistakes over and over that hurt their relationships.

Finally, the ISTP Elementary Education is Extraverted Feeling, but I have nicknamed it "Compassion." The ISTP uses this personality trait under severe stress. They react by being very insensitive, scattered, awkward around emotion, and, sometimes, emotionally manipulative.

An example of this can be an ISTP having explosive anger towards someone who does not agree with them on a particular subject.

It's important to note that there are four more personality traits that are not part of the ISTP Personality. Each Myers-Briggs type only uses four of the eight personality traits. The four personality traits of Introverted Feeling - nickname: Soul Searching, Extraverted Intuition - nickname: Theorizing, Introverted Sensing - nickname: Consistency, and Extraverted Thinking - nickname: Organization are not in the ISTP Education Model. This is because they are blind spots for the ISTP and they do not exist in their personality trait stack. There is either massive resistance or an attempt at understanding when an ISTP encounters those four personality traits that are blind spots in social interaction with another person. In other words, they are intrigued by their blind spots for better or for worse.

ISTP Career Recommendations:

- **Athlete**
- **Construction Manager**
- **Computer Programmer**
- **Mechanic**
- **Scientist**

Famous ISTPs:

- **Ashton Kutcher**
- **Clint Eastwood**
- **Kristen Stewart**
- **Scarlett Johansson**
- **Tiger Woods**

11. ESFJ

ESFJ Education Model	
PhD	Compassion
Bachelor's Degree	Consistency
High School Diploma	Theorizing
Elementary Education	Validity

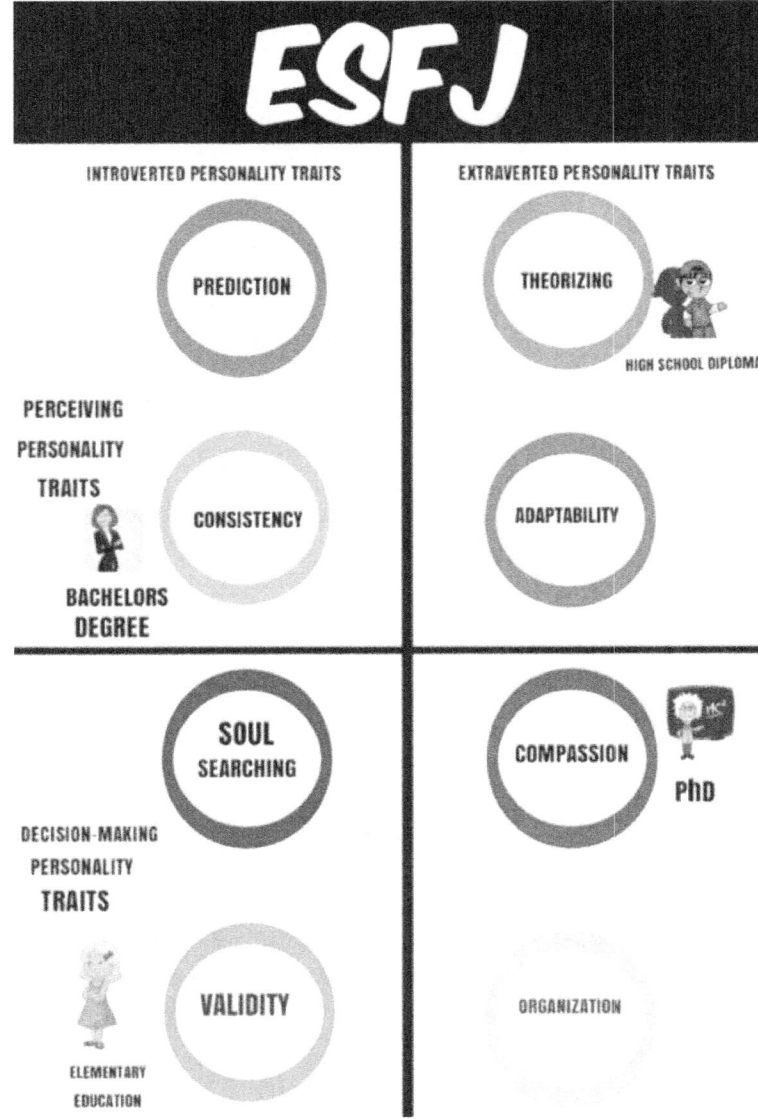

The ESFJ PhD is in Extraverted Feeling, and I have nicknamed it "Compassion." With a PhD in Compassion, the ESFJ is a metaphorical educational genius or expert when it comes to the personality trait of Compassion.

With a PhD in Compassion, they are caring and dutiful towards people's emotional needs. They are one of the two most helpful types in the Myers-Briggs personality system—with the other one being ESFJ.

ESFJs have explained that they have the uncanny ability to sense the feelings around them." This makes way for a type that has extremely high emotional intelligence.

Some great examples of this are a nurse or a teacher who are very in tune with the feelings of their patients/students. They genuinely care that everyone around them has their needs met. This can also be illustrated when this type often being overrepresented in the medical field and in education.

BACHELORS DEGREE PERSONALITY TRAIT

Their Bachelor's Degree is in Introverted Sensing, but I have nicknamed it "Consistency." With a Bachelor's Degree in Consistency, they know a fair amount about how to utilize this personality trait —it also helps them have a more integrated personality that gets them engaged in the outside world. Again, what leads to the most personal development and growth for each Myers-Briggs type is further educating their Bachelor's Degree. ESFJs have the innate sensory ability to learn from past personal experience in a constructive way. The internal senses, such as sense of time or sense of temperature, are highly developed. This, in conjunction with their PhD in Compassion, can help them remember the feelings of people around them at points in their lives. This makes them excellent friends and caregivers.

Their High School Diploma is in Extraverted Intuition, but I nicknamed it "Theorizing." We default to this metaphorical degree under stress. Another way to perceive it is that we react with the emotional maturity of a high school student when the High School Diploma personality trait is being used. Therefore, the ESFJ reacts by defaulting to the most traditional method of accomplishing something under stress. This personality trait is a weakness for the ESFJ, but the metaphorical High School Diploma of Theorizing can be further educated through personal development and growth.

An example of this is only using methods that have proven to work in the past.

Finally, the ESFJ elementary Education is in Introverted Thinking, but I nicknamed it "Validity." We default to this metaphorical degree under severe stress. Another way to perceive it is that we react with the emotional maturity of an elementary school student when the Elementary Education personality trait is being used. Therefore, the ESFJ reacts by being very divergent in their thinking, scattered, and sometimes, emotionally manipulative toward others. At times, they may even appear obsessive-compulsive in their personal and professional lives.

An example of this is the ESFJ being unnecessarily worried about things that are out of their control.

This personality trait is a weakness for the ESFJ, but the metaphorical Elementary Education can be further educated through personal development and growth. This would manifest in the ESFJ being more level-headed, "slowing down," and reflective towards others when they do not see the world as they do. Additionally, taking things "one step at a time" would further support this effort.

It's important to note that there are four more personality traits that are not part of the ESFJ personality. Each Myers-Briggs type only uses four of the eight personality traits. The four personality traits of Introverted Feeling - nickname: Soul Searching, Introverted Intuition - nickname: Prediction, Extraverted Sensing - nickname: Adaptability, and Extraverted Thinking - nickname: Organization are not on the ESFJ Education Model. This is because they are blind spots for the ESFJ and they do not exist in their personality trait stack. There is either massive resistance or an attempt at understanding when an ESFJ encounters those four personality traits that are blind spots in social interaction with another person. In other words, they are intrigued by their blind spots for better or for worse.

ESFJ Career Recommendations:

- **School Administrator**
- **Children's Daycare Administrator**
- **Nurse**
- **Salesperson**
- **Teacher**

Famous ESFJs:

- **Anne Hathaway**
- **Barbara Walters**
- **Chris Wallace**
- **Pope Francis**
- **Sarah Palin**

12. ISFJ

ISFJ Education Model	
PhD	Consistency
Bachelor's Degree	Compassion
High School Diploma	Validity
Elementary Education	Theorizing

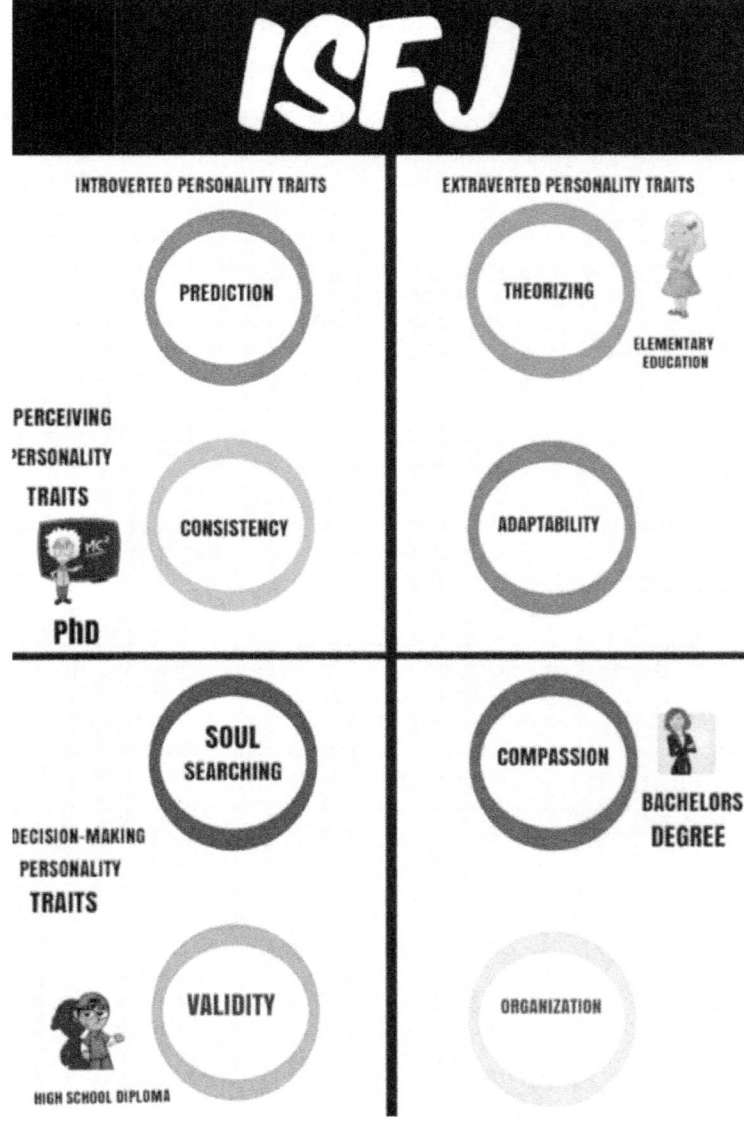

PHD PERSONALITY TRAIT

The ISFJ PhD is in Introverted Sensing, and I have nicknamed it "Consistency." With a PhD in Consistency, the ISFJ is a metaphorical educational genius or expert concerning the personality trait of Consistency.

With a PhD in Consistency, ISFJs have the innate sensory ability to learn from past personal experience in a constructive way. The internal senses, such as sense of time, sense of temperature, and sense of tradition are highly developed. This, in conjunction with their Bachelor's Degree in Compassion, can help them remember the feelings of people around them at points in their lives. This makes them excellent friends and caregivers in a more introverted way than the ESFJ.

A good example of this is an ISFJ always remembering personal holiday traditions on every holiday and finding creative ways to celebrate with other people.

Their Bachelor's Degree is in Extraverted Feeling, but I have nick-named it "Compassion." With a Bachelor's Degree in Compassion, they know a fair amount about how to utilize this personality trait —it also helps them have a more integrated personality that gets them engaged in the outer world. Again, what leads to the most personal development and growth for each Myers-Briggs type is further educating their Bachelor's Degree personality trait. They are caring and dutiful towards people's emotional needs. They are one of the most helpful types in the Myers-Briggs personality system.

ISFJs have explained that they have the uncanny ability to sense feelings around them. This makes way for a type that has extremely high emotional intelligence.

An example of this is that an ISFJ may be extremely into traditionalistic customs. They may use their PhD in Consistency to remember the routines and memories of Christmas time with their family, and then, they are able to use that in conjunction with Compassion to make the Christmas memories more meaningful each year for their family.

Their High School Diploma is in Introverted Thinking, but I nick-named it "Validity." We default to this metaphorical degree under stress. Another way to perceive it is that we react with the emotional maturity of a high school student when the High School Diploma personality trait is being used. Therefore, the ISFJ reacts by being divergent in their thinking, scattered, and, sometimes, self-obsessed. At times, they may even appear obsessive-compulsive in their personal and professional lives.

An example of this is overly obsessing on solutions to a problem that is out of their control.

This personality trait is a weakness for the ISFJ, but the metaphorical High School Diploma can be further educated through personal development and growth. This would manifest in the ISFJ being more in tune with other people's feelings, accepting the various outcomes in life, and seeking advice from friends and family to temporarily escape from their "inner world."

Finally, the ISFJ Elementary Education is in Extraverted Intuition, but I nicknamed it "Theorizing." We default to this metaphorical degree under severe stress. Another way to perceive it is that we react with the emotional maturity of an elementary school student when the Elementary Education personality trait is being used. Therefore, the ISFJ reacts by being very stubborn about sticking to what has been proven to work. They can shut down when someone discusses any sort of theory that diverges from customary behavior. This personality trait is a weakness for the ISFJ, but the metaphorical Elementary Education can be further educated through personal development and growth. This would manifest in the ISFJ being more open to spontaneity, new ways of solving problems, and healthy spontaneity in life.

It's important to note that there are four more personality traits that are not part of the ISFJ Personality. Each Myers-Briggs type only uses four of the eight cognitive personality traits. The four personality traits of Introverted Feeling - nickname: Soul Searching, Introverted Intuition - nickname: Prediction, Extraverted Sensing - nickname: Adaptability, and Extraverted Thinking -

nickname: Organization are not on the ISFJ Education Model. This is because they are blind spots for the ISFJ, and they do not exist in their personality trait stack. There is either massive resistance or an attempt at understanding when an ISFJ encounters those four personality traits that are blind spots in social interaction with another person. In other words, they are intrigued by their blind spots for better or for worse.

ISFJ Career Recommendations:
- **Accountant**
- **Children's Daycare Administrator**
- **Musician**
- **Nurse**
- **Teacher**

Famous ISFJs:
- **George H.W. Bush**
- **Kate Middleton**
- **Kim Kardashian**
- **Mike Pence**
- **Rosa Parks**

13. ESFP

ESFP Education Model	
PhD	Adaptability
Bachelor's Degree	Soul Searching
High School Diploma	Organization
Elementary Education	Prediction

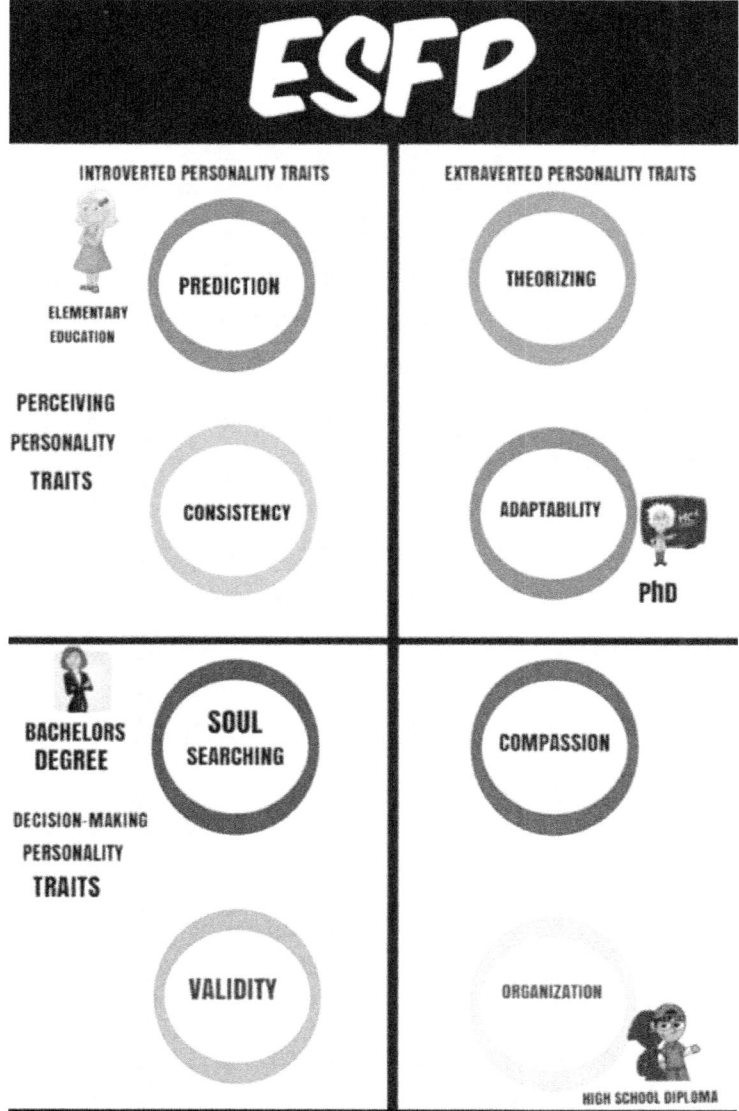

The ESFP PhD is in Extraverted Sensing and I have nicknamed it "Adaptability." With a PhD in Adaptability, the ESFP is a metaphorical educational genius or expert concerning the personality trait of Adaptability.

With a PhD in Adaptability, they love to improvise with their external senses. This includes sight, sound, touch, smell, and taste. They love using this expert awareness of these senses to try new things, be spontaneous, and seek thrills.

They have an ongoing memory of how their external senses reacted in particular situations.

Some great examples of this are riding motorcycles, improvising in a speech, working with their hands, and sports.

Their Bachelor's Degree is in Introverted Feeling, but I have nicknamed it "Soul Searching." With a Bachelor's Degree in Soul Searching, they know a fair amount about how to utilize this personality trait—it also helps them have a more integrated personality that gets them engaged in their inner world. Again, what leads to the most personal development and growth for each Myers-Briggs type is further educating their Bachelor's Degree personality trait. ESFPs have the ability to validate the sensory patterns and ideas they perceive in their PhD of Adaptability. ESFPs have the unique talent of taking the sensory insights they pick up in their external world and putting them into their own empathetic, personal value system.

ESFPs can really develop this personality trait by "slowing down" and getting in touch with their inner world about whether to make a certain decision.

An example of this is actors/actresses. Actors are able to draw patterns, insights, and intuition from observing all the different lifestyles in the world. In conjunction with soul searching, they are able to "search their souls" to find the emotions and values as to why a person chooses a particular lifestyle. Another example is an ESFP's ability to be "in touch" with their children's emotions and understand their needs.

Their High School Diploma is in Extraverted Thinking, but I nicknamed it "Organization." We default to this metaphorical degree under stress. Another way to perceive it is that we react with the emotional maturity of a high school student when the High School Diploma personality trait is being used. Therefore, the ESFP reacts by being very scattered, impulsive, anxious, and, sometimes, disorganized. This personality trait is a weakness for the ESFP, but the metaphorical High School Diploma can be further educated through personal development and growth. This would manifest in the ESFP "slowing down," investigating different options when making life decisions, and not jumping to the most straight forward solution under stress.

An example of this is an ESFP being peer pressured into participating in an unhealthy or destructive activity.

Finally, the ESFP Elementary Education is Introverted Intuition, but I have nicknamed it "Prediction." The ESFP uses this personality trait under severe stress. When this occurs, ESFPs insist that tasks are much easier to accomplish than they actually are. They spring into action without thinking about the consequences of those actions. They can become very hard-headed, foolish, and belligerent when in this state of mind.

An example of this is insisting there is only one way of accomplishing a task when there are multiple ways of accomplishing it.

It's important to note that there are four more personality traits that are not part of the ESFP Personality. Each Myers-Briggs type only uses four of the eight personality traits. The four personality traits of Extraverted Feeling - nickname: Compassion, Extraverted Intuition - nickname: Theorizing, Introverted Sensing - nickname: Consistency, and Introverted Thinking - nickname: Validity are not in the ESFP Education Model. This is because they are blind spots for the ESFP and they do not exist in their personality trait stack. There is either massive resistance or an attempt at understanding when an ESFP encounters those four personality traits that are blind spots in social interaction with another person. In other words, they are intrigued by their blind spots for better or for worse.

ESFP Career Recommendations:

- **Actor**
- **Athlete**
- **Musician**
- **Personal Trainer**
- **Salesperson**

Famous ESFPs:

- **Ariana Grande**
- **Bill Clinton**
- **Jimmy Fallon**
- **Justin Bieber**
- **Katy Perry**

14. ISFP

ISFP Education Model	
PhD	Soul Searching
Bachelor's Degree	Adaptability
High School Diploma	Prediction
Elementary Education	Organization

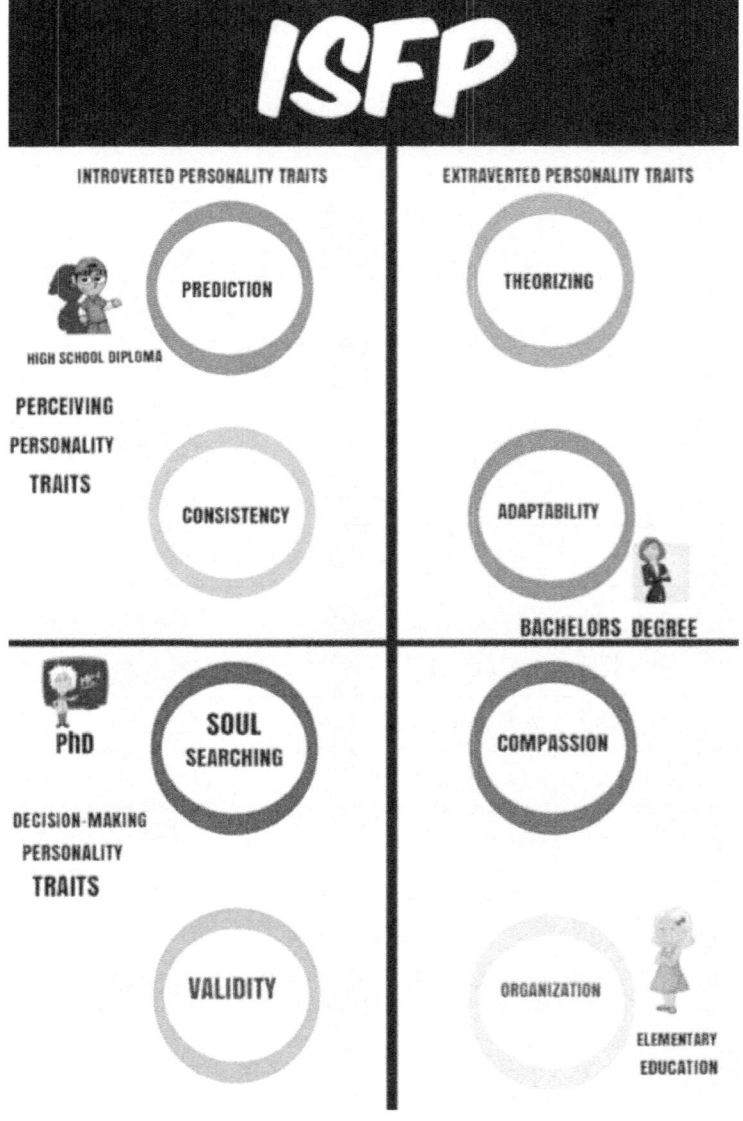

The ISFP PhD is in Introverted Feeling and I have nicknamed it "Soul Searching." With a PhD in Soul Searching, the ISFP is a metaphorical educational genius or expert in the personality trait of Soul Searching.

With a PhD in Soul Searching, ISFPs have the unique talent of being able to understand the emotions of others by being deeply introspective about their values and beliefs. They have an inherent gift of knowing "right" and "wrong" when it comes to social values. They are dreamers who stand up for their value of humanity.

An example of this is a writer who is able to write down the deepest and happiest parts of his or her mind while connecting with readers.

Their Bachelor's Degree is in Extraverted Sensing, but I have nick-named it "Adaptability." With a Bachelor's Degree in Adaptability, they know a fair amount about how to utilize this personality trait —it also helps them have a more integrated personality that gets them engaged in the outside world. Again, what leads to the most personal development and growth for each Myers-Briggs type is further educating their Bachelor's Degree. ISFPs love to produce creative work through their external senses. This includes sight, sound, touch, smell, and taste. They love using this expert aware-ness of their senses to try new things, be spontaneous, and seek creativity outlets.

They have an ongoing memory of how their external senses re-acted in particular situations.

An example of this is when they use their Soul Searching and Adaptability in conjunction with one another to create situations in which they can do creative things for others on a bad day, produce artwork that expresses themselves, and take on projects around the house.

Their High School Diploma is in Introverted Intuition, but I nicknamed it "Prediction." We default to this metaphorical degree under stress. Another way to perceive it is that we react with the emotional maturity of a high school student when the High School Diploma personality trait is being used. When this occurs, ISFP's insist that tasks are much easier to accomplish than they actually are. They spring into action without thinking about the consequences of those actions. They can become impulsive, overly focused on manual tasks as a form of escaping, and are, sometimes, emotionally isolated.

An example of this is driving the same route every day to work and expecting the traffic to lessen in intensity.

Finally, the ISFP Elementary Education is Extraverted Thinking, but I nicknamed it "Organization." We default to this metaphorical degree under severe stress. Another way to perceive it is that we react with the emotional maturity of a high school student when the High School Diploma personality trait is being used. Therefore, the ISFP reacts by being very scattered, anxious, and, sometimes, disorganized. This personality trait is a weakness for the ISFP, but the metaphorical Elementary Education can be further educated through personal development and growth. This would manifest in the ISFP investigating different mentor options when making life decisions, not jumping to the most straightforward solution under stress, and not realizing to focus on one idea at a time.

An example of this is the ISFP feeling as though they have many artistic/creative ideas, but they are overwhelmed on how they make them come to fruition.

It's important to note that there are four more personality traits that are not part of the ISFP personality. Each Myers-Briggs type only uses four of the eight personality traits. The four personality traits of Extraverted Feeling - nickname: Compassion, Extraverted Intuition - nickname: Theorizing, Introverted Sensing - nickname: Consistency, and Introverted Thinking - nickname: Validity are not in the ISFP Education Model. This is because they are blind spots for the ISFP, and they do not exist in their personality trait stack. There is either massive resistance or an attempt at understanding when an ISFP encounters those four personality traits that are blind spots in social interaction with another person. In other words, they are intrigued by their blind spots for better or for worse.

ISFP Career Recommendations:

- **Artist and/or Actor**
- **Massage Therapist**
- **Musician**
- **Photographer**
- **Teacher**

Famous ISFPs:

- **Billie Eilish**
- **Ellie Goulding**
- **Marilyn Monroe**
- **Paul McCartney**
- **Prince Harry**

15. ESTJ

ESTJ Education Model	
PhD	Organization
Bachelor's Degree	Consistency
High School Diploma	Theorizing
Elementary Education	Soul Searching

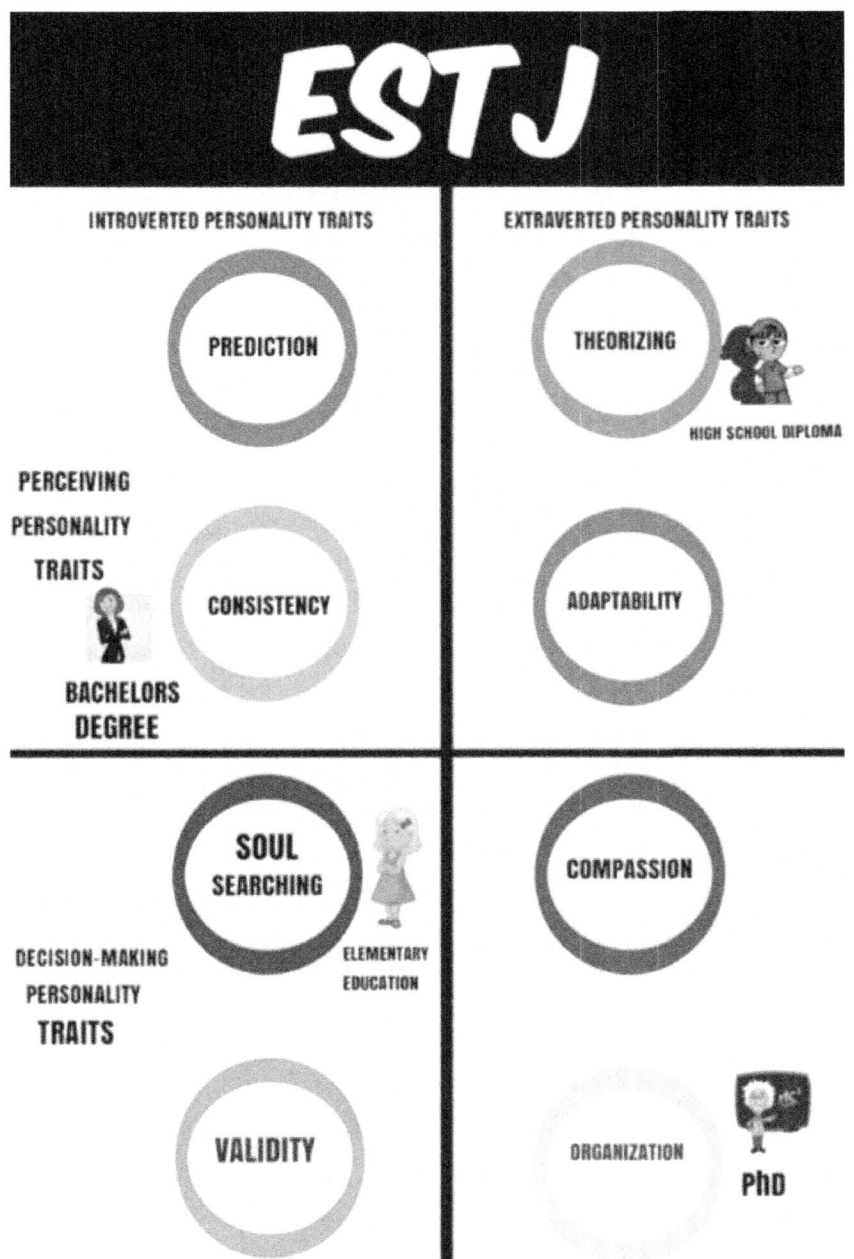

The ESTJ PhD is in Extraverted Thinking and I have nicknamed it "Organization." With a PhD in Organization, the ESTJ is a meta-phorical educational genius or expert when it comes to the personality trait of Organization.

With a PhD in Organization, they are managerial, effective, and efficient towards people's logistical needs.

ESTJs have the ability to bring order to chaos. They are logical and steadfast under pressure, and they come up with the most effective solutions to problems for people and things when dealing with logistical matters.

A good example of this is a High School Principal that is very effective and efficient at understanding where the school needs improvement. They are able to think logistically and quickly on their feet.

Their Bachelor's Degree is in Introverted Sensing but I have nicknamed it "Consistency." With a Bachelor's Degree in Consistency, they know a fair amount about how to utilize this personality trait —it also helps them have a more integrated personality that gets them engaged in their inner world. Again, what leads to the most personal development and growth for each Myers-Briggs type is further educating their Bachelor's Degree. ESTJs have the innate sensory ability to learn from past personal experience in a constructive way. The internal senses, such as sense of time or sense of temperature and sense of tradition, are highly developed. This, in conjunction with their PhD in Organization, can help them remember the logistical needs of people and things around them at points in their lives. This makes them excellent administrators and managers.

An example of this is an ESTJ manager that is able to recite the same speech word-for-word for different groups of people.

Their High School Diploma is in Extraverted Intuition, but I nicknamed it "Theorizing." We default to this metaphorical degree under stress. Another way to perceive it is that we react with the emotional maturity of a high school student when the High School Diploma personality trait is being used. Therefore, the ESTJ reacts by defaulting to the most traditional method of accomplishing something under stress. This personality trait is a weakness for the ESTJ, but the metaphorical High School Diploma of Theorizing can be further educated through personal development and growth.

An example of this is an ESTJ being afraid at work of trying anything new in their management style.

Finally, the ESTJ Elementary Education is in Introverted Feeling, but I nicknamed it "Soul Searching." We default to this metaphorical degree under severe stress. Another way to perceive it is that we react with the emotional maturity of an elementary school student when the Elementary Education personality trait is being used. Therefore, the ESTJ reacts by being severely judgmental, angry, and invulnerable.

An example of this is an ESTJ not admitting that they were wrong about something or not apologizing.

This personality trait is a weakness for the ESTJ but the metaphorical Elementary Education can be further educated through personal development and growth. This would manifest in the ESTJ "slowing down," using logical criticism instead of personal criticism, and being vulnerable to other people who can provide emotional support. ESTJs have a tendency to insist they do not need emotional support even though everyone does.

It's important to note that there are four more personality traits that are not part of the ESTJ Personality. Each Myers-Briggs type only uses four of the eight personality traits. The four personality traits of Extraverted Feeling - nickname: Compassion, Introverted Intuition - nickname: Prediction, Extraverted Sensing - nickname: Adaptability, and Introverted Thinking - nickname: Validity are not in the ESTJ Education Model. This is because they are blind spots for the ESTJ and they do not exist in their personality trait stack. There is either massive resistance or an attempt at understanding when an ESTJ encounters those four personality traits that are blind spots in social interaction with another person. In other words, they are intrigued by their blind spots for better or for worse.

ESTJ Career Recommendations:
- **Banker**
- **Business Owner**
- **Financial Planner**
- **High School Principal**
- **Salesperson**

Famous ESTJs:
- **Ben Shapiro**
- **George W. Bush**
- **Hillary Clinton**
- **Ivanka Trump**
- **Michelle Obama**

16. ISTJ

ISTJ Education Model	
PhD	Consistency
Bachelor's Degree	Organization
High School Diploma	Soul Searching
Elementary Education	Theorizing

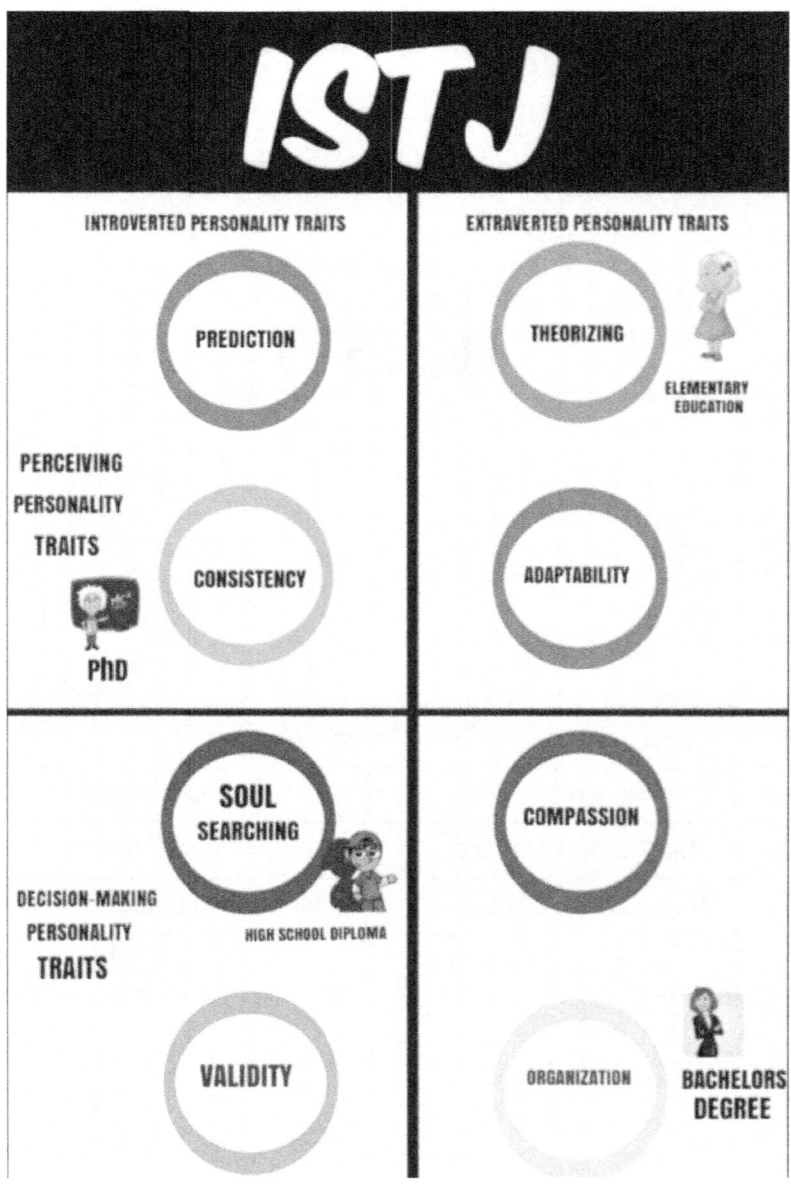

The ISTJ PhD is in Introverted Sensing and I have nicknamed it "Consistency." With a PhD in Consistency, the ISTJ is a metaphorical educational genius or expert concerning the personality trait of Consistency.

With a PhD in Consistency, ISTJs have the innate sensory ability to learn from past personal experience in a constructive way. The internal senses such as sense of time, sense of temperature, and sense of tradition are highly developed. This, in conjunction with their Bachelor's Degree in Organization, can help them remember the logistical and experiential experiences in their lives that are beneficial to their well-being.

An example of this is the ISTJ having a reputation of being excellent accountants and bank administrators in obviously a more introverted way than the ESTJ.

The ISTJ Bachelor's Degree is in Extraverted Thinking, and I have nicknamed it "Organization." With a Bachelor's Degree in Organization, they know a fair amount about how to utilize this personality trait—it also helps them have a more integrated personality that gets them engaged in their inner world. Again, what leads to the most personal development and growth for each Myers-Briggs type is further educating their Bachelor's Degree personality trait. With a Bachelor's Degree in Organization, they are managerial, effective, and efficient towards people's logistical needs.

ISTJs have the ability to bring order to chaos. They are logical and steadfast under pressure, and they come up with the most effective solution to problems for people and things when dealing with logistical matters. This, in conjunction with consistency, makes way for a type that is analytical and prone to routine-oriented schedules.

A good example of this is an ISTJ accountant who must keep up with the payroll of a company on a daily basis.

Their High School Diploma is in Introverted Feeling, but I nicknamed it "Soul Searching." We default to this metaphorical degree under stress. Another way to perceive it is that we react with the emotional maturity of a high school student when the High School Diploma personality trait is being used. Therefore, the ISTJ reacts by being severely judgmental, angry, and invulnerable.

An example of this is an ISTJ harshly judging someone for a mistake they made and letting that mistake cloud their judgment of that person.

This personality trait is a weakness for the ISTJ but the metaphorical High School Diploma can be further educated through personal development and growth. This would manifest in the ISTJ "slowing down," using logical criticism instead of personal criticism, and being vulnerable to other people who can provide emotional support. ISTJs have a tendency to insist they do not need emotional support even though everyone does.

Finally, the ISTJ Elementary Education is in Extraverted Intuition, but I nicknamed it "Theorizing." We default to this metaphorical degree under severe stress. Another way to perceive it is that we react with the emotional maturity of an elementary school student when the Elementary Education personality trait is being used. Therefore, the ISTJ reacts by being very stubborn about sticking to what has been proven to work. They can shut down when someone discusses any sort of theory that diverges from customary behavior. This personality trait is a weakness for the ISTJ, but the metaphorical Elementary Education can be further educated through personal development and growth. This would manifest in the ISTJ being more open to spontaneity, new ways of solving problems, and healthy adventure in life.

An example of this is the ISTJ not wanting to do anything differently in their daily routine.

It's important to note that there are four more personality traits that are not part of the ISTJ Personality. Each Myers-Briggs type only uses four of the eight personality traits. The four personality traits of Extraverted Feeling - nickname: Compassion, Introverted Intuition - nickname: Prediction, Extraverted Sensing - nickname:

Adaptability, and Introverted Thinking - nickname: Validity are not on the ISTJ Education Model. This is because they are blind spots for the ISTJ, and they do not exist in their personality trait stack. There is either massive resistance or an attempt at understanding when an ISTJ encounters those four personality traits that are blind spots in social interaction with another person. In other words, they are intrigued by their blind spots for better or for worse.

ISTJ Career Recommendations:

- **Accountant**
- **Administrator**
- **Banker**
- **IT Support**
- **Manager**

Famous ISTJs:

- **Angela Merkel**
- **George Washington**
- **Natalie Portman**
- **Richard Nixon**
- **Robert De Niro**

WORKS CITED

"The Myers & Briggs Foundation – Lifelong Type Development."
The Myers & Briggs Foundation – Lifelong Type Development .
Web. 11 Sept. 2015

Printed in Great Britain
by Amazon

44315475R00069